Ioway Life

The Civilization of the American Indian Series

Ioway Life

Reservation and Reform, 1837–1860

GREG OLSON

University of Oklahoma Press : Norman

Also by Greg Olson
The Ioway in Missouri (Columbia, Mo., 2008)
Voodoo Priests, Noble Savages, and Ozark Gypsies: The Life of Folklorist Mary Alicia Owen (Columbia, Mo., 2012)

Library of Congress Cataloging-in-Publication Data

Names: Olson, Greg, 1959– author.
Title: Ioway life : reservation and reform, 1837–1860 / Greg Olson.
Description: Norman, OK : University of Oklahoma Press, [2016] | Series: Civilization of the American Indian series ; volume 275 | Includes bibliographical references and index.
Identifiers: LCCN 2015041739 | ISBN 978-0-8061-5211-0 (hardcover : alk. paper)
Subjects: LCSH: Iowa Indians—History—19th century. | United States. Office of Indian Affairs. Great Nemaha Agency—History. | Iowa Indians—Government relations—History. | Iowa Indians—Land tenure—History.
Classification: LCC E99.I6 O58 2016 | DDC 323.1197/52—dc23
LC record available at http://lccn.loc.gov/2015041739

Ioway Life: Reservation and Reform, 1837–1860 is Volume 275 in The Civilization of the American Indian Series.

The paper in this book meets the guidelines for permanence and durability of the Committee on Production Guidelines for Book Longevity of the Council on Library Resources, Inc. ∞

1 2 3 4 5 6 7 8 9 10

To the Ioway people;

The *S'áge* (Old Ones), those here today
and those yet to come.

Contents

List of Illustrations   ix
Acknowledgments   xi
Introduction   xiii

1   The Long Road to the Great Nemaha Agency   3
2   "The House Is Empty"   17
3   "Useful in This World and Happy in the Next"   37
4   A Change in Ioway Leadership   60
5   Crooked Fathers and Neglected Children   81
6   Expanding Horizons and Constricting Boundaries   98
Conclusion   121

Notes   127
Bibliography   145
Index   153

Illustrations

FIGURES

The Reverend Samuel M. Irvin, Eliza Irvin, and family   23
The Wolf River, Kansas, ca. 1859   25
See-non-ty-a, an Iowa Medicine Man, 1844/1845   34
The Ioway, Sac and Fox Mission, 2014   45
The White Cloud, Head Chief of the Iowas, 1844/1845   48
Kirwin Murray, ca. 1880   53
Na'hjeNing'e (No Heart)   66
British, also known as Ragráshe, ca. 1880   77
*George Catlin and His Troupe of Iowa Performing in the
    Tuileries before Louis-Philippe and His Family*, 1845   103

MAPS

No Heart's Map, 1837   5
The Great Nemaha Subagency, 1843   27
Boundaries of the Great Nemaha Subagency (later Agency),
    1837–54   83
Boundaries of the Great Nemaha Agency, 1854–61   115
Boundaries of the Great Nemaha Agency, 1861   119

Acknowledgments

Life is a journey. So too is the process of learning about the culture, customs, and past of any group of people. I have been researching and writing about the Ioways for nearly two decades. Over that period I have come to realize that the more I know about them, the more I have yet to learn about their rich and complex story. My path to reach a deeper understanding of Ioway culture and history has led me to opportunities and possibilities I could never have imagined. For this reason, I am especially grateful for all of the people, both Ioways and non-Ioways, who have generously shared their time, research, and knowledge with me over the past several years. I have benefited significantly from their generosity and patience.

I am indebted to Cindy Peterson from the Office of the State Archaeologist of Iowa and to Saul Schwartz of Princeton University, both of whom shared their important research on the lives of the Ioways at the time they lived in and around the Iowaville site. Saul has also been helpful in leading me to source material about the Presbyterian missionaries William Hamilton and Samuel M. Irvin. Mike Dickey, the site administrator at Arrow Rock State Park in Arrow Rock, Missouri, has been a source with whom I have been able to swap information and ideas for many years. I have benefited from our exchanges. I appreciate the efforts of Dr. William Foley for his assistance in tracking down information about the Ioways' interpreter

Jeffrey Deroine. I have also learned much from my ongoing conversations with Osage elder and Newberry Fellow Larry Sellers about the broader topic of Native people and the process of colonization.

I would like to express my gratitude to several members of the Ioway community in and around the reservation of the Iowa Tribe of Kansas and Nebraska. Iowa Tribal Historic Preservation Officer Lance Foster, elder Pete Fee, and linguist Jimm GoodTracks have all been especially generous in sharing information and immersing me in the language, history, and geography of the river bottoms and Loess Hills around White Cloud, Kansas. Juli Kearns, who helps maintain various databases and websites related to Ioway language and culture, has gathered a great deal of census data, photographs, and archival records that have opened many doors to me in my research. Thanks to Dona McKinney for providing information on the Campbell and Barada families and to Sky Campbell, director of the Otoe-Missouria language program, for helping sort out nineteenth-century transcriptions of Ioway names. I have also benefited from the perspectives and information shared by Patt Murphy, Reuben Ironhorse-Kent, Sarita McGowan, Marilyn Roubidoux, Melinda Carriker, Dr. William Green, and John Palmquist.

Finally, I wish to express my appreciation to my wife, Chris, and my daughter, Tess, who have supported me through all of my many research ventures.

Introduction

In 1837 the Ioways found themselves in, what was for them, a
new and difficult situation. These Indigenous people, who as recently as
1800 had traveled freely throughout most of the present-day states of Iowa
and Missouri, were suddenly bound by the Treaty of 1836 to restrict their
living, farming, and much of their hunting activities to a two-hundred-
square-mile parcel of land. As a result of the agreement, approximately
one thousand men, women, and children were forcibly removed from the
state of Missouri and sent west of the Missouri River to the newly created
Great Nemaha Subagency in what is now southeastern Nebraska and
northeastern Kansas.[1] There, the Ioways faced a new phase of the U.S.
government's ongoing campaign to colonize them. This campaign promised the Ioways that through hard work and discipline they could gain
membership into mainstream American society. In order to attain this membership, however, the Ioways were expected to give up all that made them
Ioway—their traditional culture, religion, tribal structure, language, land,
and even their sovereignty—and to emulate the lifestyle of their white
neighbors.

For the first time in their history, the Ioways were forced to live in a
confined space that was designed and controlled by those who sought to
bring fundamental change to their way of life. Within the subagency's
boundaries the Ioways lived alongside their U.S. Indian agent, various

government employees, and Presbyterian missionaries. If the Ioways found this arrangement to be constricting, it was one their colonizers hoped to use to their own advantage. Through this shared contact, the agents and missionaries sought to manipulate details of the Ioways' daily lives—from the way they dressed to the style of their homes; from the manner in which they planted their crops to the ways they expressed themselves spiritually.

The development of Indian agencies and reservations reflected the values of American Indian policy in the nineteenth century—values guided by what we now refer to as paternalism. According to Francis Paul Prucha, paternalism was characterized by three principles. The first principle held that because Indigenous people—like European American people—had been created by God, they were endowed with the same capacities to learn, grow, and become "civilized."[2] The second principle of paternalism stated that, while Native people were physically and mentally equal to white European Americans, their cultural circumstance had rendered them temporarily inferior. As justification for this claim its supporters pointed to the so-called primitive state of Indigenous peoples' lives. While European Americans lived in an agrarian-industrial society steeped in the tenets of Christianity, Native people were viewed as mired in the state of savagism or barbarism, living as hunter-gatherers, and worshiping pagan idols. Paternalists believed that while Native people had the capacity to evolve and reach the level of civilization, they had not yet had time to rise to do so.[3]

It naturally followed that the third principle of paternalism was the belief that it was the duty of European Americans to help speed up the process of cultural evolution by guiding Native people toward civilization. In the words of Secretary of War John C. Calhoun, American Indians "should be taken under our guardianship; and our opinion, not theirs, ought to prevail, in measures intended for their civilization and happiness."[4]

At the same time, however, there existed a less optimistic discourse based in social evolution and theories of racial hierarchy that questioned Indian people's capacity to be civilized. As the Ioways settled into their new lives on the Great Nemaha Subagency, race was becoming increasingly defined by the prominent scientific theories of the day. The obsessive classification of the natural world undertaken by the scientific community gradually led to the taxonomy of human beings on a scale that measured their degree of savagery or civilization. Through such practices as anthropometry, the measurement of skull size and body proportions, scientists believed they could define degrees of intelligence and the level of civilization of the world's races. These endeavors reflected the concerns of nineteenth-century Americans over race, science, and the place of Native people in an expanding nation. These beliefs also compromised the optimistic expectation that they might ever become civilized. Skepticism over the capacity of Natives to be civilized exposed a darker side of paternalism. As Prucha points out, there was often a fine line between guidance and assistance—and between exploitation and deception. The benevolence of the parent, says Prucha, can easily lead to the oppression of the child.[5]

During the mid-nineteenth century, the Great Nemaha Subagency became a space in which these agents and missionaries turned the ideals of paternalism into practice. How successful were they at putting these theories to work? To what degree were the Ioways' lives on the subagency defined by benevolence and to what degree were they defined by oppression? And how effectively did those who operated the subagency and the mission navigate the fine line between guidance and assistance, and exploitation and deception? Most important perhaps, how successful were the agents and missionaries, during the period between 1837 and 1860, at reaching their goal of preparing the Ioways to enter mainstream American society?

In fact, the accomplishments of the agents and missionaries were decidedly mixed. Neither the subagency nor the mission enjoyed a great deal of success, at least not during the early decades of the 1840s and 1850s. Even in the restrictive atmosphere of the subagency, the Ioways were largely able to retain much of their culture while deflecting the efforts of those who tried so hard to colonize them. The Ioways seemed especially adept at accepting those items they needed from the agents and missionaries—practical things such as tools, clothing, and food—while refusing to accept their overtures of religious conversion and cultural change. It seems this resistance came from their communal skepticism about the advantages Christianity and a European American lifestyle held over their own spiritual beliefs and cultural traditions.

The Ioways' resistance was aided in no small part by the fact that the government proved largely ineffectual in its ability to operate the subagency. From the earliest days of the Great Nemaha Subagency, the government consistently demonstrated its inability to live up to the promises it made to the Ioways. Time and again, the Bureau of Indian Affairs exhibited the worst of European American cultural attitudes and values. Greed, corruption, and incompetence undermined the bureau's efforts to carry out its policy of reform and presented the Ioways with a cultural paradigm that was easy to condemn and dismiss.

Nonetheless, during this period, the agents and missionaries succeeded in planting the seeds of colonialism. Once these seeds took root, they would alter the lives of the Ioways in ways that would leave them susceptible to even greater government influence later on. Perhaps the most striking change in the Ioways' lives during these early years on the agency was their loss of self-sufficiency. The market economy had left them deeply in debt and highly dependent on the annuities they received for selling their land. Similarly, the government was able to usurp the Ioways' traditional structure of leadership, making it nearly impossible for them to govern themselves.

This book, which examines the Ioways and their struggles on the Great Nemaha Subagency, draws upon the work of a number of scholars who in one way or another have previously investigated this same topic. The history of the Ioways and the Great Nemaha Subagency has been chronicled in Martha Royce Blaine's *The Ioway Indians* (1979). Blaine was a trailblazer in identifying important primary source material, and her work is an important starting point for any student of Ioway history. As sound as her work may be, however, its broad scope (the book spans the entirety of Ioway history) leaves room for scholars who are interested in specific periods and topics to fill in details and provide historical context.[6]

One important work that followed in Blaine's wake is Joseph B. Herring's *The Enduring Indians of Kansas: A Century and a Half of Acculturation* (1990). Herring looks at the lives of the Ioways and their neighbors the Kickapoos, Potawatomis, Sacs, and Foxes as they faced initial removal and later struggle to remain in the Kansas Territory. Those nations that, like the Ioways, succeeded in retaining their land did so, according to Herring, by acculturating but not assimilating to European American culture: "They may have spoken English, farmed individual plots of land, donned overalls or calico dresses . . . but they . . . never forgot they were Indians." For the purposes of his study, Herring defined assimilation as the "complete absorption of a minority people into . . . a traditional and cultural mainstream." In contrast, Herring defined acculturation as "an intercultural borrowing that takes place when two or more diverse peoples come into close contact." While his thesis is especially helpful in the context of the study of the Great Nemaha Subagency, Herring's work, which examines at least seven different Indigenous nations, also leaves room for a more detailed exploration of the Ioways' specific experiences in territorial Kansas.[7]

Michael C. Coleman has written extensively about one of the most important influences on the lives of the Ioways during this period, the Presbyterian Board of Foreign Missionaries (BFM), which funded a number of missions throughout the world and played a crucial role in the movement to "uplift" Indian people during the mid-nineteenth century. Their mission on the Great Nemaha Subagency was one of the first the BFM established among Native people in North America. In his book *Presbyterian Missionary Attitudes toward American Indians, 1837–1893* (1985), Coleman writes about the motivations behind the Presbyterians' work. He writes that BFM missionaries pressured the Indigenous people in their missions to make changes in both their religious and social lives. "These Presbyterians could accept nothing less than . . . a cultural destruction and regeneration to be brought about by the Gospel of Jesus Christ," writes Coleman.[8] We will see this theory practiced in the work of missionaries Samuel M. Irvin and William Hamilton, who lived among the Ioways for years. While they learned much about Ioway culture and language, this exposure did nothing to sway them from doggedly pursuing their goal of bringing their own cultural and spiritual change to the Ioways.

Finally, the work of Willard Rollings has been helpful in understanding the ways in which the Ioways both resisted and accepted the influences of Euro-American culture. In his book *Unaffected by the Gospel: Osage Resistance to the Christian Invasion, 1673–1906: A Cultural Victory* (2004), Rollings discusses the Osages' similarly successful resistance in the face of their early encounters with Christian missionaries.[9]

I begin my look at the Great Nemaha Subagency with a brief overview of the relationship that existed between the Ioways and various colonial governments prior to 1836. While both Martha Royce Blaine and I have chronicled this topic in greater detail elsewhere, it is important for the purposes of this study to summarize in chapter 1 the chain of events by which, in less than forty years, the Ioways went from being a culturally independent nation that in 1800 claimed much of what is now northern Missouri and southern Iowa to a decimated people, confined to a reservation and heavily dependent on the U.S. government.[10]

In chapter 2, I discuss efforts to transform Ioway culture by examining the attempts of the Presbyterian BFM and its representatives, the Reverends William Hamilton and Samuel Irvin, to convert the Ioway to Christianity. Because their form of spirituality was an essential element of traditional Ioway culture, the missionaries' attempts to convert the Ioway constituted a fundamental challenge to their identity. In this chapter, I examine some of the ways that the Ioways were able to resist the missionary's effort to convert them. Much of the Ioways' success came from the fact that, throughout the 1840s and 1850s, they held on to their own spiritual beliefs and harbored a deep skepticism about the advantages of accepting the Bible over their own prayer bundles. As their contact with white society became more commonplace, some Ioways could not help but notice that Europeans and Americans did not always live up to the ideals of their Christian faith. This was especially apparent to the Ioways who traveled to Europe with George Catlin in 1844 and 1845. On that trip, they witnessed poverty and cruelty that seemed to contradict all the missionaries had told them about the compassion of Christ. These contradictions helped the Ioways remain convinced of the superiority of their own spiritual traditions. As a result, Irvin and Hamilton failed to win more than a small handful of Ioway converts in their long decades of mission work.

Closely related to the effort to persuade the Ioways to abandon their religion was the campaign to reeducate them. In chapter 3 I will show that on the Great Nemaha Subagency religious instruction went hand in hand with both academic and manual training and the push to encourage the Ioways to live a European American lifestyle. During the 1840s Hamilton and Irvin served as both ministers and teachers to the Ioways, and it was through their efforts that a large brick mission school was constructed on the subagency in 1845. While traditional Ioway people educated their children in a way that differed significantly from the methods used in European American schools, some Ioway leaders warily supported the idea of mission schools in order to prepare their children to survive in the white world. Perhaps for this reason, the missionaries made more progress in the mission school than they did in the chapel.

Chapter 4 is dedicated to the story of the efforts of the U.S. government to directly influence Ioway tribal leadership. While the territorial governments of the France, Spain, and Britain had all worked to win favor with Ioway headmen by awarding them medals and favoring them with privileged access to trade goods, the United States was far more aggressive in this regard. As early as 1809 President Thomas Jefferson had named the Ioway pro-American headman Hard Heart the head chief of the tribe. This meant that he alone had the authority to negotiate with the U.S. government in treaty councils. By the time the Ioway settled on the Great Nemaha Subagency, representatives of the U.S. government had learned to manipulate the distribution of treaty annuities and trade goods in a way that granted them strong influence over tribal leaders. Eventually, this influence was used to cut certain headmen such as Francis White Cloud out of their traditional tribal leadership positions. Reformers believed that Native people would benefit from the abolition of hereditary tribal leadership and encouraged them to establish an elected civil government. Over time, the Bureau of Indian Affairs succeeded in diminishing the importance of hereditary Ioway headmen such as White Cloud.

In chapter 5, I explore the problem of harmful paternalism and the persistent problems of political infighting, fraud, and corruption that plagued the Great Nemaha Subagency. Prior to their move to the subagency, the Ioways had enjoyed a relatively stable period of government representation, thanks in large part to the decade-long tenure of subagent Andrew S. Hughes. Shortly after leading the Ioways to their new home west of the Missouri River, Hughes was forced out of his position amid rumors that he was a drunk and had committed fraud. Over the next twenty years, seven politically appointed subagents passed through the subagency. While many of these subagents professed sympathy for the Ioways and expressed a sincere desire to help better their lives, most succumbed to charges—some well founded and some politically motivated—of scandal, financial mismanagement, incompetence, or fraud. Nearly all left the position of subagent unhappily. The subagents' acts of political maneuvering and financial shenanigans seem to have taken up a great deal of time and energy and seriously compromised the government's ability to effectively carry out its policy of Indian reform.

Finally, in chapter 6, I will show how the U.S. government's effort to reform the Ioways resulted in them being systematically separated from their land. Through treaties, the illegal advance of white squatters, and the forced migration of neighboring tribes, the government consistently corralled the Ioways on to ever-smaller parcels of land. Even after the tribe was removed to their two-hundred-square-mile reservation, the government continued to whittle away at the Ioways' land. This process was linked to the theory that Native people would benefit from privately owning their own land parcels. In an effort to break up village life and motivate the Ioway to become self-sufficient farmers, officials on the Great Nemaha Agency began to encourage the Ioways to accept the idea of allotment as early as 1851.

Curiously, at the same time that the Ioways were being confined to ever smaller pieces of land and were being pressured by the government to give up their traditional lifestyle, fourteen Ioway tribal members had the opportunity to travel to Europe to participate in the painter George Catlin's Indian exhibition. There, the Ioways performed the same traditional songs and dances that the missionaries and agents discouraged them from performing at home. Although some saw Catlin's exhibition as an exploitation of the Ioways, they participated willingly for the public in hopes that they could earn money and gain publicity that might help improve the poverty and indebtedness they faced at home. Sadly, even in Europe the Ioways did not receive the help they desired. Seen as enchanted children of the forest rather than as victims of paternalistic oppression, the Ioways returned home with a trunk load of Bibles and no financial aid to help them with their cause.

In the years before the Civil War, the Ioways were able to resist much of what the U.S. government and the Presbyterian missionaries tried to force upon them. However, this does not mean we should assume the period left Ioway culture unaltered. Allotment. Christianity. Acculturation. The seeds of these and other cultural institutions that eventually led to major changes in Ioway life, were planted during the first two decades the Ioways spent in the Great Nemaha Subagency.

Ioway Life

CHAPTER 1

The Long Road to the Great Nemaha Agency

Oral tradition, historical accounts, and the archaeological record indicate that the Ioways lived many places over a wide geographical area in the centuries prior to their removal to the Great Nemaha Subagency. These sources seem to agree that between the eleventh and seventeenth centuries, the Ioways—or *Báxoje*, as they call themselves—were part of a large culture we now call the Oneota. The word "Oneota" comes from a type of geological formation that is found along the Upper Iowa River, which was once called the Oneota River, in present-day northeast Iowa. In the nineteenth century, the word "Oneota" was also sometimes used as an alternate spelling for the name of the Oneida people of the Iroquois Confederacy. The Oneida, however, have no direct cultural connection to the ancient Oneota or to the Ioways. Ellison Orr and Charles R. Keyes first applied this name to an archaeological culture whose sites can be found throughout the upper Midwest.[1]

The Oneota, which had emerged as a distinct group by the eleventh century, included the ancestors of the Ioways and their Siouan-speaking relatives the Winnebagos, Otoes, and Missourias. The Oneota culture seems to have originated in the region near present-day Green Bay, Wisconsin—a place Ioways call Maya^{n}Shuje (Red Earth). Between the thirteenth and the sixteenth centuries, Oneota culture spread into parts of present day Illinois, Indiana, Iowa, Minnesota, Missouri, Kansas, and

Nebraska. Archaeologists believe this wide distribution was due in part to migration, as people spread out across a geographical area. Evidence also suggests groups of people living throughout the Midwest adopted Oneota cultural traits. Oneota people who migrated were likely forced to do so by a combination of climatic changes, disease, and the depletion of large animal populations. After 1500, the Oneota contracted diseases such as smallpox, measles, and influenza that were the tragic results of the arrival of Europeans on the North American continent. The death rate among Native people was significant enough to force survivors to realign themselves into smaller tribal alliances, which spread out in order to sustain themselves more easily. It is believed that during this time the Ioways separated from their Oneota relatives to live as a separate nation. In fact, linguist Jimm GoodTracks has posited that the name Ioway, which derives from the Dakota *Ayúxba*, was applied to them because they had "broken off" from the rest of the Oneota cultural group.[2]

To the best of our knowledge, the first Europeans the Ioways encountered were French traders and missionaries during the 1670s. At the time the Ioways were living along rivers in what is now southeast Minnesota and northeast Iowa. The first detailed European account of the Ioways comes from Father Louis André, a French missionary who met seven or eight families of Ioways at his mission at Green Bay on April 20, 1676. During their meeting the Ioways described the location of the large village in which they were living at the time. André reported two different sites for the Ioways' village. In one account he placed it two hundred leagues (about 690 miles) from Green Bay. In another, he guessed it to be a twelve-day journey west of the Mississippi River.[3] Five years later, another French missionary, Father Zenobius Membre, indicated that Ioways were living in three large villages located along either the Upper Iowa River or the Root River in present-day southwest Minnesota.[4]

Around 1685 the Ioways began to migrate west, eventually inhabiting the region between Spirit Lake, located on the border between Iowa and Minnesota, and Blood Run (now known as Good Earth State Park), which straddles the Iowa/South Dakota border near the present-day city of Sioux Falls. The Ioways made this move for both defensive and commercial reasons. At the same time the French were pushing Iroquois nations south from the Great Lakes and Canada, the Ioways faced competition from their Algonquin-speaking neighbors to the southeast, the Illinois and

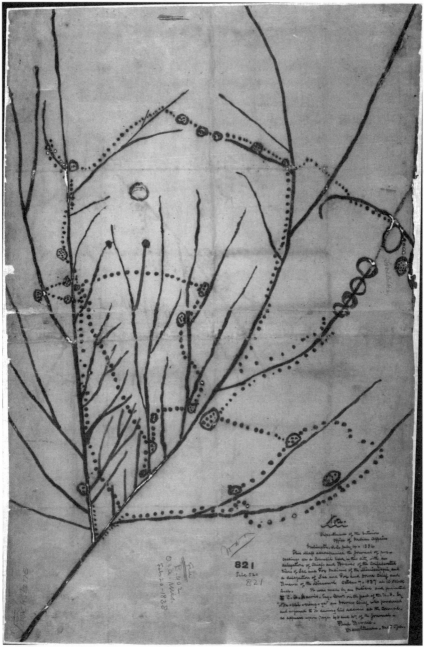

No Heart's Map, 1837. In 1837 the Ioway leader Na'hjeNing'e (No Heart), presented this map to Commissioner of Indian Affairs C. A. Harris. The map is a record of more than two centuries of Ioway village sites and migrations. The long line that runs from the bottom left to the top center of the map represents the Mississippi River. The line that runs along the left edge of the map represents the Missouri River. Circles with dots in them represent village sites and the dotted lines represent migration routes. (National Archives and Records Administration.)

the Mascoutins. After their adversaries attacked one of their villages, the Ioways moved west to be closer to their relatives and allies, the Otoes and the Omahas. Their new home near the lakes and rivers of northwest Iowa and southwest Minnesota proved to be commercially beneficial to the Ioways as well. The region's rich supply of beaver pelts helped them purchase many of the French trade goods upon which they had become reliant such as metal utensils, firearms, tools, and beads.[5]

Meanwhile, the French too had been on the move, exploring and mapping the heart of the North American continent. In February 1682 the French explorer René-Robert Cavalier, sieur de La Salle, left Green Bay to travel down the Mississippi River. On April 9 he reached the river's mouth and planted a cross and engraved plate on the bank, claiming the entire Mississippi watershed for France. In honor of the French monarch Louis XIV, de La Salle named the region Louisiana. While the Ioways were unaware of it at the time, this proclamation set in motion a process by which they and other Native nations would lose control of land on which they had lived for centuries.[6]

After 1700 the constant ebb and flow of tribal alliances and warfare kept the Ioways on the move. Conflicts between the Dakota Sioux and their relatives the Lakota Sioux, forced the Ioways away from southern Minnesota and northern Iowa. By about 1718 they had migrated down the Missouri River to the mouth of the Platte River, near the site of present-day Omaha, Nebraska. It was here that archaeologists believe the Ioways came into contact with other Plains nations who introduced them to the horse.[7] While the acquisition of the horse greatly increased the Ioways' ability to travel for purposes of war and hunting, it also increased their need for grasses and other forage to sustain their horse population. This, in turn, made it necessary for the Ioways to defend larger areas of land.

For the next several decades the Ioways moved their villages to various locations up and down a 150-mile stretch of the Missouri River between the Big Sioux River and the Platte River. Increased competition for hunting and grazing land led to conflict between the Ioways and their former allies the Omahas, Otoes, and Dakota Sioux. Afraid to hunt on their own land, small groups of Ioways migrated east toward the Mississippi River in the mid-1750s. In 1765 they sent messengers to Pierre Laclede, a fur trader who had just founded the village of St. Louis near the confluence of the Mississippi and Missouri Rivers. The Ioways asked Laclede if traders would follow them should they decide to relocate their villages to what is now southeast Iowa. After receiving Laclede's assurance that they would still have access to trade, the bulk of the Ioways soon made the trip east. As historian Saul Schwartz has pointed out, the fact that the Ioways inquired about the availability of trade before repositioning their villages shows that they were heavily involved in the market economy, and they ranked access to trade alongside military defense when choosing a home.[8]

After their move to the Des Moines and Mississippi Rivers, the Ioways came into contact with the Algonquin-speaking Sacs and Foxes. At the time the closely allied Sacs and Foxes were living on the east side of the Mississippi River along the Rock River in what is now northern Illinois. The growing numbers of white settlers strained the natural resources east of the Illinois country and forced the Sacs and Foxes to venture across the Mississippi River to hunt in the Ioways' territory. In order to maintain peace the Ioways and the Sacs and Foxes formed an alliance. The Ioways agreed to share hunting rights to their land if the Sacs and Foxes would help them defend it from other tribes. With the help of their new Algonquin allies and a supply of British firearms, the Ioways managed to retain control of their land in southeast Iowa. They also began to move down the Chariton River into the lower Missouri River valley, until they met resistance from the Osages, Kaws, Missourias, and Otoes.[9]

Although the Ioways moved often and sometimes traveled great distances to relocate their villages, they did maintain semi-permanent settlements or towns. One of the best known of these was located on the north bank of the Des Moines River in present-day Van Buren County, Iowa. From about 1784 to 1824, between 750 and 1,250 Ioways occupied this site, which is known to archaeologists and historians today as Iowaville.[10] But even during the decades the Ioways occupied Iowaville, smaller Ioway settlements were recorded, among other places, on the east bank of the Mississippi River near the mouth of the Iowa River, near Prairie du Chien, on the Upper Iowa River, on the Rock River, at the mouth of the Des Moines River, on the Grand River in northern Missouri, and on the Missouri River as far west as the Platte River.[11]

In the early nineteenth century, the Ioways claimed to control much of the land that makes up the present-day state of Iowa and the northern part of present-day Missouri. The region of Ioway influence stretched from the border between Iowa and Minnesota on the north to the Little Sioux

River and the Missouri River on the west. To the south, the Ioways claimed
territory along the Missouri River between the Grand River and the Chariton River. The eastern border of Ioway influence was defined by the Mississippi River and extended as far south as the Salt River, in what are now
Ralls and Monroe Counties in Missouri.

The Ioways believed their hold on this vast region had been so strong
that years later the headman Waich^eMáñi (the Orator) boasted, "No
Indians of any other Tribe [dared] build his fire or make a moccasin
track, between the Missouri and Mississippi Rivers . . . without first having
obtained the consent of the Ioway Nation of Indians."[12] Zachary Gussow
points out that claims such as the Orator's "cannot be accepted at face
value." It was not uncommon for Native nations to claim to control more
land than they actually did. As the Orator's statement was made during a
treaty negotiation, he may have exaggerated the Ioways' range in hopes
of winning a larger compensation for the land from the government.
Certainly, many other nations, including the Otoes, Missourias, Kaws,
Osages, Omahas, Dakota Sioux, Sacs, and Foxes all contested the Ioways'
claim. Soon, it would also be challenged by the expanding presence of the
United States, which in 1803 acquired all of the land claimed by the Ioways, and more, when they paid France fifteen million dollars for 828,000
square miles of land in a deal that became known as the Louisiana
Purchase.[13]

In 1805 the United States called a number of the Indigenous nations
living on their newly acquired land to meet with them in a series of treaty
councils. In March the United States had named the purchased land the
Territory of Louisiana and appointed General James Wilkinson, com-
mander of the U.S. military's Department of the West, as governor. In
October 1805 in St. Louis, Wilkinson and General William Henry Harrison
met with the Otoes, Missourias, Arikaras, Sacs, Foxes, Osages, Sioux, Ioways, and other nations. On October 18, 1805, twelve headmen, including
an Ioway leader whose name was recorded as Voi Ri Gran, signed a treaty
of peace and friendship with the United States. The treaty contained articles that called for all nations to cease their hostilities toward one another
and toward the United States. Should any disagreements between the
parties emerge, the treaty directed the disputing parties to bring the conflict before the U.S. government for resolution.[14]

At around that same time the Ioways began to suffer a number of setbacks that greatly lessened their influence in the region. In the first decade of the nineteenth century, a smallpox epidemic killed as much as half the tribe, leaving a surviving population of only about eight hundred.[15] In the years that followed, they were also engaged in a costly series of battles with the Osages, who lived along the southern bank of the Missouri River.[16]

Meanwhile, political loyalties began to fray the unity of the Ioway people. As the United States struggled to gain a foothold in the new territory west of the Mississippi, the British, who had long-standing trade relationships with the Ioways and other tribes along the river, fought to retain their own influence in the region. In April 1806 Nicolas Boilvin became the first U.S. Indian agent assigned to interact with the Ioways in an official capacity. From his newly established agency at the mouth of the Des Moines River, Boilvin worked to cultivate peace and friendship with the Ioways, Sacs, and Foxes.[17]

The agent's efforts notwithstanding, tensions between the United States, the British, and Native allies for both sides escalated over the next few years, culminating with the War of 1812. Many Native people in the Mississippi River valley viewed the war—and an alliance with the British—as an opportunity to resist the Americans. During that conflict the Ioways split their allegiances. In 1813 a pro-American faction of Ioways, led by their head man Wyingwaha (Hard Heart), separated from others in the tribe who had sided with the British. The pro-British Ioways remained near the Des Moines and Mississippi Rivers and joined the Sacs and Foxes in fighting the Americans. Ioways participated in notable attacks on U.S. military posts on the Mississippi River, on the Missouri River settlement of Cote Sans Dessein, and on a small fortification near the mouth of the Chariton River known as Cooper's Fort.

Meanwhile, at the urging of famed explorer and U.S. general William Clark, Hard Heart's band moved west, away from the fighting, to settle along the Grand River in north central Missouri. This move left the pro-American Ioways open to attacks from Poncas and Omahas, who lived nearby. Even though the group expressed their allegiance to the Americans, Manuel Lisa, a trader who was acting as a U.S. Indian agent, incited a group of Yanktoni Dakotas to attack Hard Heart's Ioways. As a result, many Ioways died and their crops were burned and destroyed.[18]

At the conclusion of the War of 1812, the United States once again sum-
moned the Ioways and eighteen other Native nations to a treaty council at
Portage de Sioux, near St. Louis. Understandably, the Ioways were wary
of meeting with the U.S. officials, let alone becoming their allies. Both the
nation's pro-British and pro-American factions had suffered at the hands
of the United States. Defeated, the Ioways, led by Hard Heart, signed a
treaty of peace and friendship with the United States on September 16,
1815. During the council, the Ioways surprised government agents by offering to cede some of their land. It is difficult to know what to make of
this seemingly spontaneous offer. Did the Ioways make the offer as a goodwill gesture to prove their allegiance with the United States, or did they
do so in hope of receiving annuity payments and protection from the U.S.
military? While the treaty commissioners, trader Auguste Chouteau, governor of the Illinois Territory Ninian Edwards, and Missouri Territorial
governor William Clark, advised the President James Madison to accept
the offer, the government ultimately did not.[19]

Sometime between 1819 and 1824, the Ioways left their home at Iowaville. Violence with the Sacs and Foxes—perhaps precipitated in part
over a joint lead-mining operation or by encroachment on the Ioways'
hunting land in 1818—forced the Ioways out of their Des Moines River
villages.[20] A legend that has remained popular for nearly two centuries
contends that in May 1819, the Sac and Fox headmen Black Hawk and
Pashepaho led a surprise attack on the town while the Ioways were engaged in a celebration. Some nineteenth-century accounts estimated that
the Ioways lost as much as one-third of their total population of one
thousand men, women, and children in the attack. Modern historians
who have studied the village site and the nineteenth-century population figures for the Ioways are skeptical about reports of such huge losses.
The report seems to be based on the account of a single person, trader
James H. Jordan, which was printed by historian A. R. Fulton in the
1880s. Jordan's tale aside, there is no historical evidence to support the
story of the massacre. What is clear is that the Ioways abandoned the village site, moving south to live in what is now northern Missouri, and that
the Sacs and Foxes continued to occupy the Iowaville site after the Ioways
left.[21]

For several years, the Ioways inhabited the river valleys of the Platte,
Grand, and Chariton Rivers. In 1821 most of that land became part of the

new state of Missouri. As the state government and settlers began to challenge the Ioways for use of the land, the Ioway headmen MaxúThka (White
Cloud) and MániXáñe (Great Walker) agreed to the first-ever cession of
Ioway land to the United States. In 1824 Superintendent of Indian Affairs
in St. Louis, William Clark, accompanied the two leaders to Washington
to meet with President James Monroe and Commissioner of Indian
Affairs, Thomas L. McKenney.

McKenney had been appointed by Secretary of War John C. Calhoun
earlier that year to lead the newly formed Bureau of Indian Affairs and
to supervise its two employees in Washington. At the time U.S. Indian policy focused on two main objectives. The first was to remove Native people
west of Missouri to a designated Indian territory in order to separate them
from white settlers. Violence with settlers and the corrupting influences
of unscrupulous traders and whiskey dealers had left many tribes destitute,
including the Ioways. The government believed that separating Natives
and settlers could solve many of these problems. The United States was
also eager to gain clear title to all of the land inside Missouri's borders to
which Natives still held a claim.[22]

The government's second objective was to "civilize" Indigenous people
so that they could learn to function in European American society. William Clark expressed the feeling of many at that time when he reasoned
that, if Native people were afforded the opportunity to own their own
property and could learn to farm and manufacture objects in the same
manner as their white neighbors, they could pull themselves out of the
poverty into which many of them had become mired. "Property alone,"
wrote Clark, "can keep up pride of an Indian and makes him ashamed of
his drunkenness, begging, lying, and stealing."[23]

During the 1824 treaty negotiations White Cloud was not eager to relinquish land, pointing out that the Ioways had been "deceived by the
Spaniards and the French for they had no right to the country which they
sold to the Americans." Recognizing, however, that their people did not
have the power to contest the United States' possession of the land, he and
Great Walker agreed to sell all of the Ioways' rights to the northern half
of Missouri for five thousand dollars. The treaty also provided the tribe
with a blacksmith, agricultural tools, and cattle, which the government
hoped would induce the Ioways to renew their pursuit of agriculture and
allow them to become self-sufficient.[24]

Since the Treaty of 1824 stipulated that the Ioways were to vacate the state of Missouri by 1826, the land that lay between the state's original western border and the Missouri River was designated as Indian territory. As such, the land was supposedly off-limits to white settlers. The War Department also established an agency, which the Ioways shared with the Missouri River band of the Sacs and Foxes, on the banks of the Platte River near the site of the present town of Agency, in Buchanan County, Missouri.[25]

White Cloud led the majority of the Ioways to live near the new agency, but a minority of about sixty refused to follow him. That group trekked north and east with Great Walker to live on the Chariton River near Missouri's northern border. After returning from Washington, Great Walker came to believe he had made a mistake in signing the Treaty of 1824. The Ioways had lived and hunted in northern Missouri for decades and their Oneota ancestors had occupied the land centuries before that. Many of Great Walker's people had been buried on that land, and in the end, he could not abandon them. Painting his face as a sign of his regret and mourning, he told government officials, "I am ashamed to look at the sun. I have insulted the Great Spirit by selling the land and the bones of my fathers; it is right that I should always mourn."[26]

Great Walker technically followed the letter of the Treaty of 1824. His intention was to keep his people north of the Missouri border and occupy land the Ioways still held claim to in present-day Iowa. However, his "pouting party" as settlers pejoratively called them, ignored the spirit of the treaty by refusing to live on the land the government had set aside for them along the Missouri River.

The leader's resistance led to bloodshed in July 1829, after Great Walker and some of his men discovered several newly constructed settler cabins. The cabins were located just west of present-day Kirksville, Missouri, near the Chariton River and well south of the Missouri line, but Great Walker believed they were on land the Ioways still rightfully claimed. The Ioways warned the settlers that if they did not move, the U.S. military would force them to do so.

Afraid that the Ioways had violent intentions, the settlers raised a small militia to confront them. On July 17, 1829, the armed settlers visited Great Walker's camp in present-day Schuyler County, Missouri. A gunfight broke out in which three Ioways and three settlers were killed. Eventually, Great

Walker and twelve other Ioways were arrested and tried for murder in Huntsville, Missouri. In the trial, the jury acquitted the Ioways because they believed that, even though the skirmish had taken place twelve miles south of the Iowa-Missouri border, the Ioways were defending themselves on what they believed to be their land. In fact, at that time, even the state of Missouri was unsure about the exact location of their northern border. A poorly worded constitution left the boundary ill-defined and nearly led to war with the Iowa Territory a decade later. Not until the 1850s did the U.S. Supreme Court settle the border confusion.[27]

Meanwhile, the United States had begun the process of gaining the rights to Ioway land north of the Missouri border. In 1825 Superintendent of Indian Affairs in St. Louis William Clark and governor of the Michigan Territory Lewis Cass held a treaty council at Prairie du Chien with the Ioways, Sacs, Foxes, Sioux, Ojibwas, Winnebagos, and representatives of other Native nations. Clark and Cass had called the council to persuade the various tribes, all of whom were struggling to maintain their own territories, to end their hostility with one another. The end result, however, was that each tribe in attendance plotted the land it claimed on a map. The government told the Native delegates that partitioning the land and recording each nation's claims in the treaty would serve to keep them peacefully separated. In fact, the document helped the government determine which nations they needed to pressure in order to get the land cessions it desired. At Prairie du Chien, White Cloud and nine other Ioway headmen agreed to peacefully share their land in southeast Iowa with the Sacs and Foxes.[28]

This set the stage for a subsequent council at Prairie du Chien with many of the same nations five years later, just weeks after the Indian Removal Act had passed Congress on May 28, 1830. In that treaty, signed by White Cloud, Ñi'yuMa'ñi (Raining), Péchaⁿ (Crane), and seven other Ioways, all tribes attending the council ceded the western portion of the present-day state of Iowa to the United States. The cession also included the Platte River country between the Missouri state line and the Missouri River, the land on which the Ioway Agency was located. In return, the United States promised to pay the Ioways twenty-five hundred dollars and provide them with a blacksmith and agricultural tools for a period of ten years.[29]

During the treaty council, both White Cloud and Crane expressed their desire to follow the advice of the government. White Cloud proclaimed that he was ready to lay down his weapons and went as far as to declare, "look upon me and you look upon almost a white man." Later, however, the Ioways claimed that, because they had not been supplied with a translator, they had not understood the terms of the treaty they signed. Claiming they had not intended to cede their claim to western Iowa, the Ioways would continue to contest that treaty until 1837.[30]

The treaty also set aside a tract of Otoe land on the west side of the Missouri River for the exclusive use of mixed-race Ioways, Omahas, Otoes, Yankton Sioux, and Santee Sioux. Historian Tanis Thorne has pointed out that this so-called half-breed tract, which had been proposed at the council by the Mdewakaton Sioux leader Wabasha, was a "concession to traders," many of whom fathered children with Native women. The tract was intended to be a place where mixed-race Natives could establish farms, but the tract remained largely uninhabited until after the Kansas-Nebraska Act opened the land west of the Missouri River to white settlers in the 1850s.[31]

Several mixed-race Ioways eventually moved to the Nemaha Half-Breed Reservation and seventy-two received allotments of land there when the reservation was broken up in 1860. The Ioway patriarchal clan system created a problem for mixed-race offspring. Clan affiliation came from the father. When Ioway women bore children of non-Native men, the offspring had no clan affiliation and therefore no place in traditional Ioway culture. Some tribal members adopted these children into their clans, but many were left in a cultural no-man's land in which whites considered them Native and Natives considered them white.[32]

As the state of Missouri grew in population, settlers and politicians alike began to covet the Indian Territory between the Missouri River and what was then the state's western border. Although the area had been part of the Ioway land cession in the Treaty of 1830, confusion surrounding just what the Ioway understood about the agreement left the cession in doubt. Settlers were eager to own the area's rich farmland, while business interests wanted access to that section of the Missouri River located between present-day Kansas City and the Iowa line. Members of Missouri's congressional delegation had discussed annexing the territory as early as

1829. In December of that year, Senator Thomas Hart Benton and Congressman Spencer Pettis wrote to Secretary of War John Eaton asking the Bureau of Indian Affairs to meet with the Ioways, Sacs, Foxes, and other nations living in the Platte country for the purpose of making a treaty to relinquish it. "[The land] is essential to the State of Missouri," declared Benton, "and hardly desirable to the Indians on account of its narrowness."[33]

In 1831 Missouri's General Assembly petitioned the U.S. Congress, requesting that no additional tribes be assigned to live in the Platte country. In Congress, Missouri Senator Lewis Linn led the campaign to extend the state's western border to the Missouri River once all Indian rights to the land could be terminated. As early as 1828 several Ioway headmen met with their subagent, Andrew S. Hughes, to discuss selling their claim. The Ioways were not opposed to selling their land along the Platte River as long as money from the sale could be used to send Ioway children to be educated in white schools.[34]

In September 1836 the Ioways traveled to Fort Leavenworth with Subagent Hughes and the leaders of the Sacs and Foxes of the Missouri for a treaty council led by Stephen Watts Kearney. The headmen ceded all their rights and claims to the land between the state of Missouri and the Missouri River to the United States for seventy-five hundred dollars. The treaty stipulated that, within a year, the Ioways, Sacs, and Foxes would be moved to two separate land reserves of two hundred square miles each on the south bank of the Great Nemaha River on the border between present-day Kansas and Nebraska. The treaty, which became known as the Platte Purchase, granted the Ioways five "comfortable houses." The government also agreed to fence off two hundred acres of land, which would be prepared for cultivation. The treaty promised that the Ioways would receive tools, 205 head of cattle and hogs, and a year's worth of food rations, as well as the instruction of a schoolmaster, a farmer, and a blacksmith.[35]

The following March, President Martin Van Buren issued a proclamation allowing the state of Missouri to annex the Platte River country. In the late spring of 1837, the Ioways, Sacs, and Foxes made the trek across the Missouri River to an uncertain future on their new homeland. In roughly four decades, life for these Native people had shifted dramatically. The

Ioways, who in the year 1800 claimed much of southeast Iowa and north-ern Missouri, were now confined to a four-hundred-square-mile reserva-tion. With the loss of their land would come other challenges. Ioway tradi-tions of education, spirituality, economics, and culture, all of which were tied to the land, were forever altered. The Ioways would have to find new ways to live in their new home.

CHAPTER 2

"The House Is Empty"

What is to become of these poor Indians? Is there no blessing
in store for them? The enemies of God triumph and glory
in their shame, trampling under foot the laws of God and
man. Why are they permitted to lead these ignorant souls astray,
sinking them deeper in degradation and sin, by their contaminating influence?

The Reverend Samuel Irvin, 1841

Ioway people were no strangers to European Christianity when
they arrived at the Great Nemaha Subagency in 1837, for 161 years earlier in 1676 "seven or eight families" from the nation had traveled to Green
Bay, in present-day Wisconsin, to visit their relatives the Winnebagos and
to conduct business with French traders.[1] There they met a French Jesuit
priest named Louis André who operated a mission. André queried the Ioways about the location of their village and the wealth of their nation and
he "preach[ed] Jesus Christ to them."[2] We do not know how deeply André
delved into Christianity during what was likely a brief visit with the Ioways.
Similarly, we do not know how they reacted to the priest's sermon. What is
certain, however, is that André's preaching offered the Ioways a worldview
that was markedly different from their own.

According to William Hamilton, a Presbyterian missionary who would
live among the Ioways for eighteen years, while the Ioways often spoke of
their God, they were "ignorant" of the true character of the Christian God.
They referred to Ma^un (the Creator of the Earth) whom they also referred to as Waka^nda (Supreme Being) or Hintuga (Grandfather). But the
Ioways also told Hamilton that the sun, the moon, the winds, and the
Thunder Beings that lived in the West were Waka^ndas. One Ioway man
told Hamilton there were seven Waka^ndas in all.[3] The Ioways' tradition of
seeing the sacred manifestations of the Creator in the world around them

highlights the main difference between their worldview and that of European American Christians. Christians saw the natural world as a place over which God had directed them to exercise control. The Ioways saw themselves as a part of the natural world.

The Ioways understood that they had come from the mother earth, which they called Hina Maya, and they believed that the animals, birds, plants, and earth itself were their relatives. In the Ioways' language, the word for "being" (*wan^shige*) is used when speaking about both humans and animals.[4] The Ioways saw the many different wan^shiges in the world, but they believed that all had a purpose and all were equal to one another. According to the Ioways' oral tradition, the first wan^shiges that wandered the earth—the four-legged, two-legged, and winged ones— had the ability to communicate with one another as well as with plants and insects. Later, when some of the four-legged beings transformed themselves into humans, they retained some animal characteristics and kept the ability to communicate with their nonhuman relatives. It was from these early part-human beings that the Ioways clan ancestors were said to have descended.[5]

Philosopher and historian Carolyn Merchant has described the worldview of the Ioways and other Native people as a "participatory consciousness." Merchant writes that for Indigenous people, no "sharp boundary existed between humans and their animal ancestors. . . . No separation between mind and body, thinking subject and passive object, animal and resource as yet existed. . . . The natural and spiritual were not distinct."[6] This outlook was evident in nearly all the Ioways' day-to-day activities. Farming, for instance, was an activity that required interaction between many beings. The Ioways knew centuries-old ceremonies that encouraged Hina Maya's cooperation in bringing seeds to life. According to the Ioways' oral tradition, the buffalo clan had introduced corn (*waduje*) to the people. Therefore, before the women could plant corn in the spring, buffalo clan leaders and healers held ceremonies asking the corn's assistance in feeding the people. As they planted corn, beans (*honyi*), and squash (*wadwan*), the women sang to the seeds to encourage them to grow. They called upon the sun and the thunder beings to help bring a successful harvest so that the people might live another year.[7]

Merchant contrasts the participatory consciousness of Indigenous people with the "mechanistic consciousness" of European Americans. This view of the world sprouted from the seventeenth-century theories of René Descartes, Thomas Hobbes, and Sir Isaac Newton, who conceived of the human body, the earth, and the heavens as distinct parts of a machine that worked together in a natural order. Merchant argues that the United States' founding fathers adapted this mechanistic language in discussing the "machine of government" and the importance of its harmonious workings. Coupled with the Puritan belief in a biblical directive to exercise dominion over nature, European mechanistic consciousness helped to legitimize man's domestication of the environment and the quest to civilize the continent through Manifest Destiny. Merchant writes that the "mechanical, instrumental view of nature was subtly legitimating and advocating its management and manipulation."[8]

In the decades just prior to the Ioways' removal to the Great Nemaha Subagency, Christian denominations in the United States felt a strong desire to promulgate their religion and values among Indigenous people in North America and abroad. This desire was fueled by the Second Great Awakening, which historian Willard Rollings has described as an "outburst of public piety . . . which became a national evangelical movement inspiring thousands of Americans to flock to churches and outdoor gatherings to hear a new message of Christian salvation." This awakening was a rejection of the harsh formalism of Calvinism, which taught that salvation was only for a select few. Instead, Baptist and Methodist clergy embraced the idea that all who believed in Christ could be saved. These preachers, who came from a broad base of lay people rather than from elite seminaries, shared their democratic message of salvation in a language that could be understood by all.[9]

During this period, many American Christians believed God had specially selected their new nation to be the springboard for a Christian civilization that would cover the entire world. To accomplish this aim, evangelicals sought to Christianize every aspect of moral, spiritual, and intellectual life. Protestants in particular began to organize a variety of voluntary organizations aimed at spreading the tenets of the new Christian society. This work had a particular urgency because many believed the approaching millennium marked the time when Christ would return to earth to begin his thousand-year reign. With the millennium less than two hundred years away, Christians faced the pressing challenge of preparing all the people of the world, especially the uninformed heathens, for Christ's return. These Christians believed that once heathens heard the word of Christ, they would discard their own cultures for salvation. To this end Christian missionaries fanned out across the globe to Africa, India, Asia, and to Indigenous peoples across North and South America.[10]

Although wary during their first encounters with missionaries, some Ioways began to allow their children to be educated in Christian schools after the land on which they lived became a part of the United States. The Ioway headmen White Cloud and Great Walker agreed to send boys to St. Regis, a Jesuit school in Florissant, Missouri, near St. Louis. The school formally opened its doors on May 11, 1824. One month later three Ioway boys arrived at St. Regis in the company of their parents and Ioways' agent Gabriel Vasques. The agent warned the school's headmaster, Father Charles Felix Van Quickenborne, he would need to watch the boys closely as they were likely to flee. In fact two of the boys did make at least one attempt to escape, but the priests quickly returned them to the school. One of the Ioway boys was Great Walker's thirteen-year-old son, who remained at the school long enough to be baptized and given the name Peter in 1825.[11]

Before the 1830s the Ioways' exposure to Christianity had been sporadic. All this changed when Presbyterian missionaries came to live among them in 1835. Presbyterians had ministered to Native people since 1741, when Azariah Horton moved to Long Island to preach to Indigenous people there. In the first two decades of the nineteenth century, Presbyterian missionaries began to work with the Cherokees and Choctaws. After the Presbyterian Church of the United States of America (PCUSA) split along theological lines in 1837, the more conservative "Old School" wing of the church established the Board of Foreign Missionaries (BFM) to oversee the mission work of church members. The conservative Presbyterians believed that it was the church's business to ensure that Presbyterian missions throughout the world operated as a "well organized army."[12]

The new BFM inherited a Presbyterian mission for the Weas and Piankeshaws in present-day Miami County, Kansas, as well as a fledgling mission for the Sacs, Foxes, and Ioways. In 1835 the Presbyterians had dispatched missionaries Aurey Ballard and E. M. Sheppard, and teacher Nancy Henderson from the Wea mission to the old Ioway Agency in what is now Buchanan County, Missouri.[13] As the Ioways, Sacs, and Foxes traveled across the Missouri River to the site of the new Great Nemaha Subagency in 1837, the BFM made plans to locate a new permanent mission near their villages. Ballard and his wife made the move to the site of the new subagency, but poor health forced him to retire after a few months. In the spring of 1837 the Reverend Samuel Irvin and his wife, Eliza, joined the Ballards. The Reverend William Hamilton and his wife, Julia, arrived at the new station in December. These missionaries were among the first foot soldiers in an army of Presbyterians that the BFM dispatched to nineteen Indian tribes between 1837 and 1893. At its height this army of missionaries would number nearly 450 men and women.[14]

The purpose of the BFM was to help Native people become "civilized, self-supporting people [who were] prepared to take upon them the duties of full citizenship." The BFM planned to accomplish this by implementing four goals. First, they wanted to send missionaries to the various tribes for the purpose of preaching the gospel to them. Second, the BFM wanted these missionaries to create a self-supporting "native ministry among the heathens." To help implement these first two goals, the BFM sought to translate the Bible and other religious texts into Native languages. Finally, the BFM vowed that it would bring Native people, especially young children, a "common education." This education had three main components: religious teaching, vocational training, and academic instruction. The Presbyterians believed that only through this broad instruction would Native people be fully prepared to accept the privileges and responsibilities of citizenship in the United States.[15]

Presbyterian missionaries believed that Native people had the capacity to reach this goal but had been prevented from doing so by their cultural circumstances. While they believed that Native people were repressed by a culture that forced them into a state of heathenism, the missionaries were nonetheless convinced that individuals had the capacity to rise above their savage state. The historian Michael Coleman contends that, as a group, these missionaries were given to a condescending and paternalistic view of the Indian people, largely because they could only view Native culture through the narrow lens of their own ethnocentrism. This perspective left them confident in the superiority of European American Christian civilization and led them toward the conviction that every aspect of traditional Native culture had to be destroyed in order to free Native people and make them ready be saved.[16]

Coleman has noted that Presbyterian missionaries reflected the BFM's Old School conservative outlook. They tended to be well-educated middle-class people from small communities who answered the BFM's call out of a romanticized sense of patriotism and denominational pride. These recruits threw themselves wholeheartedly into their mission of transforming the nation's Indigenous population and, in doing so, winning the world for Christ. The longest-serving missionaries at what came to be called the Ioway (or Iowa), Sac and Fox Mission at the Great Nemaha Subagency, Samuel Irvin and William Hamilton, both conformed to this general description.[17]

A native of Lycoming County, Pennsylvania, William Hamilton was just twenty-six years old when he arrived at the Great Nemaha Subagency in December 1837. Though young, he had already been a member of the Presbyterian Church for a decade. Not only was he well educated (he had attended both college and seminary), he had two years of teaching experience and was already an ordained minister.[18] Samuel M. Irvin had also received religious training by the time he arrived at the subagency from Pittsburg, Pennsylvania. A year younger than Hamilton, Irvin was described as a frail, sickly man who had been warned by doctors that the trip west would compromise his already fragile health. In fact Irvin would die near the subagency—but not until 1887, when he was seventy-five years of age. Both men arrived at the mission with young families (Hamilton's wife, Julia Ann McGiffin Hamilton, was pregnant when they arrived at the mission), but they seemed committed to facing the hardships and uncertainties that lie ahead.[19]

During the years the two men spent at the mission, their primary contact with the BFM was the board's corresponding secretary, Walter Lowrie. A native of Scotland, Lowrie moved with his family to the United States at the age of seven and eventually settled in Butler County in western Pennsylvania. While still a young man, Lowrie set aside thoughts of going into the ministry and became a politician. After serving in both houses of the Pennsylvania legislature he was elected to the U.S. Senate in 1818. Lowrie served just one term as a senator but stayed in Washington, where he held the post of secretary of the Senate for eleven years. Tired of the high drama of capitol politics and having recently lost his wife and one daughter, Lowrie resigned his post to work with the newly created BFM in 1836. Between 1837 and 1863 when the Ioway, Sac and Fox Mission

The Reverend Samuel M. Irvin (*right*), Eliza Irvin (*center*), and their children. (Kansas State Historical Society)

closed, Irvin and Hamilton exchanged hundreds of letters with Lowrie. During that time he served as a mentor, confidant, and source of moral support to the two missionaries, who often felt lonely at their isolated outpost some nine hundred miles away from their Pennsylvania homes. Lowrie was a strong force in moving the BFM's program of practical education for Native children forward and could, when necessary, be called upon to lobby his former colleagues on Capitol Hill on the board's behalf.[20]

Hamilton and Irvin learned much about the Ioways during the decades they spent living among them. They became fluent in the Ioways' language and acquired a great deal of knowledge about their culture and spiritual beliefs. Both missionaries also displayed a great deal of compassion, paternalistic though it may have been, for the Ioways as people. They tended to the sick, aided those who needed help, and often intervened on the Ioways' behalf to ensure that trades and business dealings with whites were fair. The missionaries wrote often of their worries about the health, welfare, or sobriety of individuals within the tribe. Nonetheless, they held fast to their own core convictions where Christianity was concerned. For them there was never any doubt about the inferiority of the Ioways' traditional way of life. The missionaries believed that the quicker the Ioways chose to abandon their wretched and savage ways the sooner would come the day of their salvation.[21]

To facilitate their program of salvation, Irvin and Hamilton initiated what Michael Coleman calls "an assault on almost every aspect of aboriginal Indian culture." This assault was thorough and trickled down to the smallest details of domestic life. Irvin reported, "Indian children have everything to learn, even how to sit on a bench, or a chair—to hold the knives and the fork at the table—to wear our style of clothes—and even how to wash the face and dry it with a towel."[22] Yet their new station provided them with few tools to aid them in undertaking what seemed to them to be a monumental task.

Perhaps the most immediate challenge the missionaries faced upon their arrival at the subagency was the complete lack of accommodations and facilities. The government had been eager to remove the Ioways, Sacs, and Foxes expeditiously from the Platte country, but they had failed to make any preparations for their arrival on the new subagency. Isaac McCoy had been late in surveying the lines separating the Sacs' and Foxes' land from that of the Ioways. This in turn led to delays in locating sites on which to build much-needed permanent facilities. The tribes, who had arrived in the spring of 1837, built their initial villages roughly a mile from one another, near the spot where the Wolf River emptied into the Missouri River. McCoy completed his survey of the subagency's boundaries in early August. The survey included land set aside for the mission three miles west of the Wolf River on a rise between the Iowa Branch, now called Mission Creek, and Striker Creek. This made it possible for Irvin to oversee the construction of two log houses before winter. By November 1, 1837, the Irvins has settled into one of the houses. The second was ready for the Hamiltons when they arrived in December.[23]

The missionaries began their work modestly by holding church services and classes in one of their log homes or in the lodges of their Ioway neighbors. By 1841 the inventory of mission buildings included not only a third log house, which was occupied by missionary Henry Bradley and his wife, but also a small school building. At some point the missionaries began to

The Wolf River, Kansas, ca. 1859 (oil on canvas), Albert Bierstadt (1830–1902). During an 1859 trip artist Albert Bierstadt visited this camp along the Wolf River in the Kansas Territory. The painting evokes a time two decades earlier when the Ioways, Sacs, and Foxes had settled along the river upon their arrival at the Great Nemaha Subagency. (Detroit Institute of Arts, USA / Founders Society purchase, and Dexter M. Ferry Jr. fund / Bridgeman Images.)

operate a small farm, which provided food for the mission and work experience for the boys at the school. Still, Irvin lamented the fact that improving their accommodations had proved to be slow. "Our facilities are poor and we are perhaps more poor in improving them," he wrote in 1842.[24]

It was not until October 1842 that Irvin and Hamilton organized a church at the mission. It is not clear where the worshipers met, though the congregation's membership of just seven individuals allowed for meetings to be held in the school or in one of the missionary's homes. Hamilton noted that the modest assembly was initially made up of members of "the mission family," namely, the Irvins and Hamiltons. Samuel Irvin's brother Francis, who worked for both the mission and the subagency as a farmer, became the church's ruling elder. Among those who petitioned to be baptized in the new church were the mission teacher, Nancy Henderson, and a local African American girl named Harriet Wallace. The congregation allowed at least one Ioway member, a girl who had been raised in the Irvin household, to join them. Unfortunately, Hamilton did not include the girl's name in his reminiscences of the church's early years. The missionary's comments hint that, while other Ioways sometimes participated in church services, only the unnamed girl became a permanent member of the church.[25]

In 1843 Subagent William Richardson drew a detailed map of the Great Nemaha Subagency and the mission. McCoy's seemingly arbitrary survey line dividing the Sacs and the Foxes from the Ioways ran about two miles southwest from a bend in the Wolf River and then due west for about three miles to the site of the present-day town of Highland, Kansas. Richardson's map locates the mission just north of the survey line and the agency just south of it. Members of both tribes moved their villages south, away from the Missouri River, in order to escape the mosquitoes that plagued the lowlands near the river. The relocation also placed them closer to the mission and the subagency buildings. Richardson indicated that in 1843 there were three buildings on the mission property, though he did not label them on his map. Perhaps these are the same three log structures included by the missionaries in their 1841 inventory.[26]

At the time the Ioways lived in two separate villages. About one mile north of the mission, near the road leading to the Missouri River ferry at a landing known as Iowa Point, was Neumonya, or Raining's village.

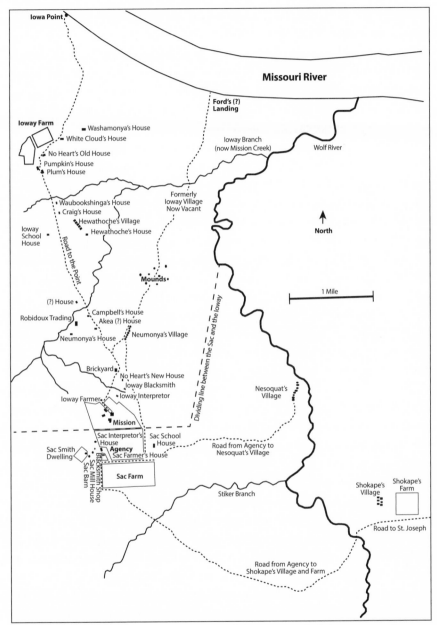

The Great Nemaha Subagency, 1843. This map, copied from one subagent William Richardson prepared in 1843, shows the location of the agency buildings, the farms of the Sacs, Foxes, and Ioways, and the location of a number of homes and villages. (Map by the author. Copyright © 2016, University of Oklahoma Press.)

Raining and No Heart lived in dwellings nearby. A mile farther north was a village that Richardson labeled Hewathoche's village. About half a mile beyond that, near the Ioways' farm, were homes belonging to the Ioway leaders, Plum, Pumpkin, and Francis White Cloud. The Sacs and Foxes also lived in two main villages. Nesoquat's village was located east of the mission on the west bank of the Wolf River. Shokape's village was a mile south of that, on the far side of the Wolf River.

In 1845 the missionaries finally started construction of the crown jewel of their missionary efforts: a large, three-story boarding school. The Ioways, the Sacs and Foxes, the U.S. government, and the BFM jointly funded the brick building, a portion of which still stands today. At 102 feet by 36 feet, the new school accommodated manual training classes and academic and religious instruction, with enough room to board between seventy-five and one hundred students, though it generally operated at less than half that capacity. (The boarding school and its role in educating the Ioways will be discussed in more detail in the next chapter.)

Even with the new school, funding for the mission remained a constant source of concern. Irvin and Hamilton were regularly forced to plead with their supervisors in Pittsburg for sufficient funds and supplies to operate their station. In one letter written in July 1851, for example, Irvin informed Walter Lowrie that the fences around the mission farm and the school playground were in terrible shape, the barn and stable both needed new roofs, the few oxen and horses that had survived the previous winter were old and incapable of fieldwork, the cook stove was broken beyond repair, and the gristmill had long since ceased to function.[27]

Facilities were not the only obstacle hindering the missionaries plan to convert the Ioways, Sacs, and Foxes to Christianity. In the early years of their tenure the missionaries were hampered in no small part by the fact that they arrived on the reservation with little or no knowledge of either the Ioways' Siouan language or the Sacs' and Foxes' Algonquin tongue. Just prior to the Hamiltons' arrival in December 1837, the mission's lone interpreter had been murdered. Until his dismissal in 1841, a former slave named Jeffrey Deroine worked as a government interpreter for the Ioways. While Deroine may have occasionally assisted the missionaries as an interpreter, it is also likely that they used his services only when absolutely necessary. Irvin, Hamilton, and the Great Nemaha's Subagent Richardson distrusted Deroine and suspected him of having undue influence over the Ioways and of being a bootlegger. "Efforts to instruct [the Sacs, Foxes and Ioways] in the truth of the gospel were . . . [unsuccessful] as the service of a capable interpreter could seldom be obtained," Hamilton recalled years later.[28]

Both Hamilton and Irvin sought to solve the language barrier by learning to speak Ioway. One of their teachers was likely a mixed race man of Ioway descent named Elisha P. Smith, a Christian who had been educated by the retired missionary Aurey Ballard. After Subagent Richardson dismissed Deroine from his duties as interpreter, he hired Smith to take his place. Irvin's progress in learning the language must have been swift, because on January 1, 1843, Richardson hired him to succeed Smith. This put Irvin in the position of being an employee of the Bureau of Indian Affairs and of the Board of Foreign Missionaries simultaneously. He served as both interpreter and missionary to the Ioways until September 17, 1844, when Richardson hired John Baptiste Roy as the new Ioway interpreter.[29]

Knowledge of the Ioways' language helped the missionaries accomplish the BFM's stated goal of translating the Bible and other religious texts into the native languages of the Indigenous people they served. In 1842 Hamilton and Irvin requested a printing press from the BFM. The board approved their request and the press arrived at the mission in April 1843. Irvin reported that they were at work translating the gospels of Matthew, the first eleven chapters of the book of Genesis, and the Ten Commandments before the press was even delivered. A year later, he noted, "The only works yet printed at the mission press, are a hymn book, and some elementary books for the school. These have been found of great assistance, and when other works are prepared and printed, they will encourage the adult Indians, as well as the youth and children to learn to read."[30] By 1845, Irvin was able to report progress in the mission's press:

> The small printing press has been found of much advantage to this mission. The works printed in the native language are; an elementary book of 100 pages; a hymn book, 62 pages; a book of prayers, 24 pages; a catechism, 30 pages. Part of the New Testament is translated, and ready for the press. The children learn to read in their own language with great ease, and it is found to be an inducement and an aid in learning English. The parents, also, are often deeply interested in hearing their children read in their mother tongue.[31]

Irvin's enthusiasm about the success of the mission's self-published books was likely overstated for the benefit of his supervisors in Pittsburg. While the Ioways were more tolerant of the missionaries' attempts to convert them to Christianity than the Sacs and Foxes had been, they were no more accepting. Irvin and Hamilton tried to reach them in a variety of different ways. They invited the Ioways to attend church services on Sunday morning and prayer meetings on Wednesday evenings. They also conducted daily worship—presented in the Ioways' language in the morning and in English in the evening. Regardless of whether the missionaries held these services at the mission or in the Ioways' villages, they proved of limited success. Some Ioways would occasionally attend, sit politely throughout the meeting, and leave without a word. Just as often they would quietly leave before the service was finished. On rare occasions, Ioways would disrupt the meetings, and on at least one occasion the disruption turned violent. In September 18 a brother of the headman KáxeThka (White Crow) assaulted Hamilton by pulling his hair and striking him while he preached.[32]

On Tuesdays and Fridays the missionaries visited Ioways in their lodges. Often these visits included ministering to the sick. In the winter of 1842 the Ioway leader Kánje (Plum) was sick and near death. He accepted regular visits from Hamilton and Irvin during his final weeks. Plum liked to hear the missionaries talk about God but told them he was "ignorant" of Christian ways. He said that he suffered so much he welcomed death and was at peace with it. When the missionaries informed him that, unless he prayed to "God to cleanse his soul," his spirit would continue to suffer after he died, he asked them to pray for him. The missionaries asked Plum why he did not pray for himself, to which the old man replied that he did not know how.[33]

Other Ioways were less welcoming and found ways to gently resist the missionaries when they came calling. After allowing Irvin or Hamilton to enter their lodges, some Ioways would dominate the conversation so completely that the missionaries did not have the opportunity to turn the topic to God. Others would permit the missionaries to enter their lodges only to ignore them as they continued with their daily chores. Still others would make a point of lying down to take a nap in front of the visiting clergymen. On many occasions the missionaries did not make it past the lodge entrance. After finding out the object of the missionaries' visit some residents would ask them to go elsewhere. Some Ioways refused them entry by flatly stating, "the house is empty."[34]

The challenge for the missionaries seemed to be significant. Many Ioways simply did not accept that Christianity was superior to the spiritual practices that had helped them for centuries. Furthermore, they could not overlook the contradictions they observed between Christianity's teachings and the less than exemplary way in which many Christians conducted themselves.

When the missionaries talked about the importance of the Bible, Ioways would often counter that much of their spiritual and ceremonial lives revolved around their sacred bundles and pipes. The Ioways had many bundles, each belonging to a different clan or group and all used for different purposes. There were bundles for war, healing, tattooing, and for taking power away from the Ioways' enemies. Sacred bundles might contain animal skins, feathers, herbs, small stones, rattles, and whistles, all wrapped in a deer hide. When not in use, individual Ioways would hang their bundles in a tree or from a stick near their lodge. Sometimes they placed them on top of their bark lodges or inside in a corner.

According to one traditional story, the Ioways received the original sacred bundles from Doré and Wahrédua (the Twin Holy Boys). These twins were responsible for making it possible for humans to live in this world. They had harnessed the power of the Thunder spirits and vanquished the Waru'ska (the Giants) and killed the Ihdo'pahin (Sharp Elbows), who had previously made the world a dangerous place. After making the world safe, the twins embarked on a journey to visit the four corners of the earth. As part of this journey Wahrédua visited the World Above, where the spirits gave him each of the war and medicine bundles that the Ioways would need for later use. At each of the four directions, the twins visited clan ancestors who instructed them on making the clan war bundles. The Ioways routinely refused the missionaries' requests that they exchange their bundles for Bibles, stating that the bundles had protected and served them well in all phases of their lives.[35]

The Ioways also kept their *ráhnuwes* or sacred pipes in hide bags. They used these pipes to pray, offering tobacco to the directions as they filled them. The American author Bayard Taylor related an incident in which one of the fourteen Ioways who traveled to Europe in 1844 to meet the painter and showman George Catlin used his pipe for prayer while sailing from New York to Liverpool aboard the packet *Oxford*. Taylor reported that at one point in the crossing, the winds died and the Ioways "began to be fearful we were doomed to remain there forever, unless the spirits were invoked for a favorable wind." One of the Ioways, whom Taylor called the Prophet, smoked his pipe and prayed to the winds. "Then, having obtained a bottle of beer from the captain, he poured it solemnly over the stern of the vessel into the sea. There were some indications of wind at the time, and accordingly the next morning we had a fine breeze, which the Iowa[y]s attributed solely to the Prophet's incantation and Eolus' love of beer."[36]

The Ioways had many questions about Christianity. They professed to be confused by the fact that not all white man held the same religious beliefs and that there were more than one kind of Christianity. This especially impressed the fourteen Ioways who traveled to Europe. These travelers had the opportunity to meet with a number of clergymen who were eager to speak to them during their two-year tour. The headman Hears Intermittently, whom Catlin called the War Chief, was particularly interested in religion and talked with Methodists, Baptists, Roman Catholics, Jews, and Anglicans, among others, about their beliefs. This led Francis White Cloud and WašíMáñi (Fast Dancer)—Catlin referred to him as Jim—to tell the War Chief jokingly that he needed to buy a black coat like the missionaries wore, as "they expected [him] . . . to preach white man's religion when he got back" to the subagency.[37]

The party made light of what they came to call "the six religions of the white man." Raining's ten-year-old son, Wéxawìrugraⁿ (the Commanding General), rendered an elaborate drawing that depicted long lines of stick figure Christians ascending to heaven via six extended ladders—each ladder representing a different Christian denomination.[38] At the foot of each ladder, a larger stick figure representing a member of the clergy assisted the smaller figures as they began their journey. Another line of stick figures in the General's drawing inch toward a clergyman who throws them into a large fire that is meant to represent hell. Interestingly, the General drew a separate ladder by which the Ioways ascend to their own heaven, which was unconnected to that of the whites.[39] The War Chief explained this reflected his belief that:

We do not think your religion good, unless it is so for white people, and this we don't doubt. The Great Spirit has made our skins red, and the forests for us to live in. He has also given us our religion which has taken our fathers to "the beautiful hunting ground," where we wish to meet them. We don't believe the Great Spirit made us to live with pale faces in this world, and we think He has intended we should live separately in the world to come.[40]

The Ioways struggled with the missionaries' teachings about the concepts of heaven and hell, sin and retribution. These tenets of Christian thought were foreign to them, as was the biblical cosmology that placed heaven in the sky and hell below ground in a fiery pit. One of the Ioways asked Irvin if there was not some danger that someone making the long climb up to heaven might fall and be seriously hurt. Another wanted to know who stoked hell's big fire.[41]

While visiting the Zoological Garden in London, ThíNádaye (Blistered Feet), whom Catlin called the Doctor, discussed the concept of hell with a clergyman who accompanied the Ioways for the outing. When the reverend expressed surprise that the Doctor had heard of hell, the Ioway replied that he had learned about it from the black coats who lived among them back at the subagency. When the reverend asked the Doctor if he believed in hell, he admitted he was not certain. He told the minister there might be such a place for white people. In fact, he had heard there was at least one hell located under the streets of London. But the Doctor doubted that Ioways went to such a place when they died.[42]

The Ioways observed that there was often a stark contrast between Christianity as it was preached and Christianity as it was practiced. While visiting the English city of York, the two sites that most impressed the Ioways were the cathedral and the prison. They saw the former as a symbol of the white man's ingenuity but found the latter to be a place of great degradation and wickedness. They were further horrified when they learned that many of the prisoners were serving time because they could not pay their debts. Wouldn't it be better to simply kill these prisoners, rather than allow them to languish in prison? the Ioways asked. "When a man is dead he is no expense to anyone," they reasoned. "His wife can get a husband again, and his children a father to feed and take care of them. When he is in jail, they must starve."[43]

See-non-ty-a, an Iowa Medicine Man, 1844/1845 (oil on canvas). George Catlin (1796–1872). See-non-ty-a was also known as ThíNádaye (Blistered Feet). Perhaps because he was a medicine man, George Catlin called him the Doctor. Catlin reported that the Doctor spent much of his time in London and Paris making observations about the manners, customs, and religions of European people. (Paul Mellon Collection, National Gallery of Art.)

The Ioways could not help but notice the number of "gin palaces" they saw while touring the streets of London. This perplexed them, because the missionaries Hamilton and Irvin had often preached to them at home about the evils of alcohol. Likewise, Catlin had done his best to steer the Ioways away from drinking establishments while they were on tour. The Ioways wondered why, if alcohol was evil, the whites allowed so many businesses to engage in selling it. In an attempt to quantify the number of sinful grog shops in London, the Doctor counted each one he saw one day during an hour-long carriage ride. When he reported his findings to his traveling companions, they responded with disbelief. They decided to make a trip from St. James's Street to Blackwall, and back again, counting the shops together along the way. They laid down their bets and set off on a carriage to retrace the route and record the tally. In all, they counted 754 gin palaces on their drive. Even after Catlin discounted 300 as being apothecaries, the final count stood at an impressive 454.[44]

Another tally that led the Ioways to question the generosity of Christians was the number of Parisian women they observed on the streets who led "little dogs on strings," or leashes. During a one-hour drive in Paris, the Doctor counted more than six hundred women with little dogs. This seemed odd to the Ioways, especially given that they had seen so many poor children in the streets during their European tour. This led the Doctor to wonder if the whites did not care for their little dogs more than they cared for their children.[45]

Observations such as these led many Ioways to doubt that Christianity offered them a way of life in any way superior to their own, and most initially remained wary of adopting it. As a result the mission failed to make an impact on the spiritual lives of the Ioway people. In reviewing the failure of Christians to convert the Ioways' Siouan relatives the Osages in the nineteenth century, historian Willard Rollings observed, "the missionaries asked too much, and gave little in return, and as a result they failed." Essentially, this sums up the efforts of Irvin, Hamilton, and the others who toiled away at the Ioway, Sac and Fox Mission. The Presbyterians offered the Ioways little that was useful to them, so they were tolerated—but largely ignored. The Ioways appreciated the missionaries' supplies of tools and medicine, and they sometimes sought their assistance in dealing with the government or other white institutions. However, the missionaries' religious teachings were of little practical use to the Ioways, so the teachings failed to take root in the Ioways' daily lives.[46]

Yet despite their apparent failure to convert the people of the subagency, both Hamilton and Irvin remained dogged in their determination to carry the mission forward. They steadfastly defended themselves against those who suggested their time among the Ioways, Sacs, and Foxes had been wasted. Even those who are brought up in the church, they argued, often did not give their hearts to God in just twelve or fifteen years. As Irvin had written in the late 1830s, "Faith and patience are as much required on the part of Christians in their efforts to benefit the North American Indian, as in their labors for the people of any other part of the heathen world."[47]

In 1850, a decade and a half after the Presbyterians first began their mission, Hamilton admitted, "The preaching of the Gospel has, as yet, produced no visible marked effect." He added that the Ioway, Sac and Fox Mission had "perhaps, always been the most discouraging of all the stations of the Board [of Foreign Missionaries], and the most trying to their faith."[48]

CHAPTER 3

"Useful in This World and Happy in the Next"

Education was an important part of the Presbyterian Board of Foreign Missionaries' attempts to help Native children become "civilized, self-supporting people, prepared to take upon them the duties of full [U.S.] citizenship." As James B. Ramsey, the head of the Presbyterian academy at the Choctaw mission, professed, teachers must do more than simply pass knowledge on to the Native students. They must prepare them to be "useful in this world and happy in the next." But just as the Christian approach to spirituality proved difficult for the Ioways to comprehend and follow, European American styles of education seemed to run counter to the Ioways' customary modes of teaching and learning.[1]

In traditional times Ioway children learned the life skills they needed by watching and helping adults with their daily tasks. Young boys and girls assisted women with farming, cooking, and tending to domestic chores. As they grew in age young girls learned about tending crops. Agriculture was the domain of women, who prepared the fields in the spring, planted seeds, and tended to the crops until it was time to harvest. Women also learned to make cloth, tan hides, and produce the tools and implements needed in their daily tasks. Young boys learned to hunt and trap small animals. The Ioway leader No Heart remembered shooting squirrels with a bow and arrow when he was a child. As a young man, he hunted deer and elk with a gun.[2] Young men also joined war parties—first as helpers and later as active participants. By taking part in these activities the children learned from their elders so that they could perform the work on their own when the time came. In this way young Ioways studied how to master the knowledge necessary for their people to thrive.

Ioways also taught important lessons about their history, traditions, and principles through stories they told in their lodges and camps. Ioway oral literature is divided into two basic types, *Wekan* and *Worage*. Wekan are those stories that have to do with the sacred and the distant past. These tales can only be told in the fall and early winter when the sun is making its way southward in the sky. Wekan stories are populated by heroes such as Mischinye (Rabbit), old man Ishjinki, or Doré and Wahrédwa (the Twin Holy Boys). In some of these tales the heroes confront evil beings such as Ihdo'pahin (Sharp Elbows) and Waru'ska (the Giants). The manner in which the heroes prevail against the evil ones contain teachings about the importance of virtues, customs, social order, and the struggle between good and evil. Because the characters in Wekan stories can change form and communicate with other creatures and beings, the stories also teach about the kinship among humans and other beings that inhabit the natural world.[3]

In one story, for example, a small insect decides to play a trick on old man Ishjinki. The insect hides itself on a *yethri* plant and calls out to Ishjinki, daring him to eat the plant, which is known to act as a laxative. Thinking it is the plant rather than an insect that is taunting him, proud Ishjinki boasts that he can eat it without feeling its effects. "I've done it before and I can do it again. Nothing happens." He eats part of the plant and says to it, "Now make me ease myself." Soon, however, Ishjinki is overcome with a bout of diarrhea so severe that he ends up covered in his own excrement and manages to rub some in his eyes. Unable to see, Ishjinki must grope his way to a nearby river to wash. Because his vision is impaired the old man relies on native trees to act as his guides. When he stumbles upon an oak tree, he knows that he is on the high ground overlooking the river. Later he bumps into an elm and realizes that he is getting closer to the river's bank. Feeling a cottonwood he knows he is very close to his destination. Finally Ishjinki finds a willow, which he knows grows at the edge of the river he was so desperate to find. Imbedded in this story is practical information about the medicinal properties of plants and knowledge of where on the landscape certain trees tend to grow. The story also contains lessons about the consequences of giving in to one's vanity.[4]

Worage stories, which can be told throughout the year, take place in the time after humans appeared on earth. Historian and linguist Jimm GoodTracks has pointed out that these tales are often based on historical facts and describe incidents in which humans receive "some intercession or aid rendered by the spirit world." Holy beings from Wekan tales sometimes appear in early Worage stories, but most relate to humans and their struggles with vanity, passion, and other weakness. These stories also teach about the importance of maintaining balance and ethical behavior.[5]

In one example a man kills his wife and tricks his son and daughter into eating some of her cooked flesh. While the children discover the truth about their mother's fate, the man sneaks away to another village where he marries the headman's daughter. The son and daughter follow their father to the new village. When they arrive the father tells the villagers that the children are bad and have killed their mother. He directs the villagers to build boats and make an escape. When the boats are ready some men glue the children's eyes shut while they are sleeping. While boy and girl are incapacitated the villagers sneak away, leaving the children on their own.

Grandmother mouse comes to the siblings' aid by licking the glue away from their eyes. As soon as they are able to see, the children rush to the shore to find all the boats and villagers gone. On the shore they meet another grandmother who provides them with food and provisions. Over time the son becomes a skilled hunter and the daughter marries a man who is equally good at hunting. As the three prosper they learn that the rest of the villagers are in a bad way and that many have died. The three invite all to return to the village, promising that they will share their bounty with everyone except their father. As the people return, life returns to normal and everyone does well, except for the father who is banished by the people for his evil deeds. This story teaches children about traditional codes of morality and justice.[6]

The Ioways' traditions of teaching stand in stark contrast to European American methods of classroom education. The tension between those two approaches in education played out in a variety of ways as Ioway children began to attend Christian schools in the 1820s. As we have seen, the Ioways sent a few of their children to Christian schools fifteen years before their removal to the Great Nemaha Subagency. The five Ioway boys who attended St. Regis, the Jesuit school near St. Louis, actively resisted their education at the beginning of their stay.[7] Although Father Pierre-Jean DeSmet, a young teacher at St. Regis in 1824, described the Ioway boys as "very attentive," he related that they did not adapt easily to life at the school. Not only did two of the Ioway boys attempt to leave the facility, all the boys had a hard time adjusting to the school's strict daily schedule. They had to work in the fields each day for several hours. Farming did not appeal to them because in their culture it was traditionally the work of women and children. The Ioway boys were approaching the age at which they would normally be learning to hunt and to become warriors. Father Charles Felix Van Quickenborne, who established St. Regis, reported they "all wept when the hoe was put into their hands for the first time." Another teacher at the school remarked, "It had constantly to be impressed upon the boys that manual labor was not a thing to be ashamed of."[8]

After a few months away from home, the boys' behavior progressed in a way that pleased their white teachers. In January 1825 Father Van Quickenborne reported that a group of Ioway leaders returned to St. Louis for a meeting with William Clark. During their stay in the city several of the Ioway students traveled into the city to visit the headmen. The boys "were well dressed and behaved extremely well," Van Quickenborne wrote later. "On entering the city one of them drove the cart in which the others [rode], which amazed the Indian fathers exceedingly. They were highly satisfied and General Clark, I have been told, said after the talk was over, to the Agent: 'I wish all the Indian boys were with Catholics.'"[9]

After St. Regis closed in 1831 White Cloud accompanied a group of Ioway students to the Choctaw Academy in Blue Springs, Kentucky. The school was far away from their home, but it appears a small number of Ioways attended the school into the 1840s. According to Swiss artist Rudolph Friedrich Kurz, the Ioways referred to the academy as Johnson's School after its founder Richard Mentor Johnson. When Kurz stayed among the Ioways in the late 1840s he was surprised to find that some of the young men spoke fluent English. They told him that Mr. Johnson was a "great friend to the Indians." Ioway boys who attended the academy learned trades and became shoemakers and tailors. Kurz believed this training "ruined them as Indian braves," because the boys had no prospect of work and no longer fit in once they returned to their people. These

Ioways "became the most unhappy, the most indolent, and the most disregarded among their people."[10]

In the meantime the government sought to bring a European American style education to as many Native children as possible. They contracted with religious organizations such as the Presbyterian Board of Foreign Missionaries to establish and operate schools in Native communities. As early as 1818 the congressional House Committee on Indian Affairs had proposed a program of manual training and education for Native children. A year later Congress appropriated ten thousand dollars for an Indian Civilization Fund, which it distributed to missionary organizations.[11] Methodists and Baptists are credited with organizing the first mission schools in present-day Kansas. The Reverend Thomas Johnson and his wife, Sarah Davis Johnson, occupied the Shawnee Methodist Mission around December 1, 1830, in present-day Johnson County. About that same time Isaac McCoy, who later surveyed the boundaries of the Great Nemaha Subagency, gained permission from the Shawnees to establish a Baptist mission nearby. By 1834 several missions had already been established for Native people. The Baptists operated missions for the Shawnees and Delawares while the Methodists had teachers living among the Peorias, Shawnees, Delawares, and Kickapoos. There were also government teachers living among the Delawares and Kickapoos.[12]

In early 1834 the Presbyterians established a mission school for the Weas and Piankeshaws, who had been removed the previous year from Indiana to present-day Miami County, Kansas. One year later teacher Nancy Henderson began dividing her time between the Wea Mission and the Ioway Agency in Missouri. Soon after the Ioways' move to the Great Nemaha Subagency, another teacher from the Wea Mission, Rosetta Hardy, arrived to help missionaries Samuel Irvin and William Hamilton establish a mission school there. By 1838 the BFM added a mission school for the Chippewas and Ottawas in Grand Traverse Bay, Michigan. Eventually, the BFM would operate nineteen schools for Native children in the United States.[13]

On the Great Nemaha Subagency, the Sacs and Foxes had refused to attend the missionaries' religious services. They also chose not to send their children to the Presbyterians' mission school. "The Sacs show no willingness to have their children taught, and care little for any intercourse with the missionaries," Hamilton and Irvin reported in 1839. Although the Ioways did not reject them outright the missionaries admitted that "to obtain their full confidence is a difficult matter." Nonetheless, the missionaries believed that Native people had the capacity to change. Irvin's and Hamilton's writings indicate that they believed the Ioways, Sacs, and Foxes lived as they did because they did not discriminate between those whites who meant to help them and those, like the whiskey traders, who robbed and cheated them. "Why are [the whiskey traders] permitted to lead these ignorant souls astray," the missionaries asked, "sinking them deeper in degradation and sin, by their contaminating influence?" Irvin and Hamilton viewed the Ioways as children who were overly susceptible to the influence of outsiders. The missionaries' optimism for the eventual civilization of the Ioways was rooted in their belief that they would one day choose to follow the missionaries' positive influences over those of the other, less scrupulous whites that surrounded them.[14]

For the first seven years of their tenure at the mission Irvin, Hamilton, and the mission teachers taught in the most primitive of facilities or in no facilities at all. In 1841 Irvin noted in his diary that he was teaching in a bark lodge to which he had to attach a temporary door to keep out inclement weather. That same year Congrave Jackson, the Ioways' subagent, listed a schoolhouse on an agency building inventory. Jackson did not include any details about the building's construction or size but assessed the value of the structure at $150—which is equal to about $3,500 today—far less than any of the other buildings listed on the mission's inventory. By 1843 Subagent Richardson included two school buildings on a map he drew of the subagency. There was a school for the Sacs and Foxes, which was located just a half mile east of the mission. Given their refusal to attend classes, it seems doubtful that the Sac and Fox school was used for its intended purpose. Richardson also indicated there was an Ioway school three miles north of the mission, near the homes of No Heart, White Cloud, and other Ioway headmen.[15]

The missionaries struggled to overcome the resistance of the Sacs, Foxes, and Ioways to accepting their instruction. The BFM had transferred two teachers, Henry Bradley and Rosetta Hardy, from the Wea Mission to the Ioway, Sac and Fox Mission for the purpose of teaching in the Sac school. After two years of waiting unsuccessfully for the Sacs' and Foxes' attitude toward the missionaries to soften, Bradley and his wife moved on to the Chippewa Mission in Michigan and Ms. Hardy returned home to Pennsylvania. On September 23, 1841, the subagency hired William Hamilton to be the teacher at the Sac and Fox school. It appears Hamilton was no more successful in attracting students than his predecessors had been. Two years later the position of teacher for the Sacs and Foxes disappeared altogether from the role of those employed at the subagency.[16]

In the early years a number of teachers passed through the Ioway, Sac and Fox Mission. Because of the isolation and the harsh conditions, they did not often stay long. When others were not available to teach at the school, the missionaries stepped in to work with the children. However, gathering willing students for classes often proved a challenge. While many Ioways were simply unwilling to subject their children to European American education, those who were willing found that regularly scheduled classes often conflicted with the rhythms of traditional life. In the early days the missionaries scoured the reservation villages each day for pupils. Often upon their arrival, they would find that many prospective students were away. "Went to teach but found the village nearly emptied," Irvin wrote one day in April 1841. "They had all went up to [No Heart's] to the great Scalp Dance which was to be celebrated there. I got seven scholars who did well, the rest being absent." Often, students were called away for hunting or to work in the fields.[17]

Once he had succeeded in persuading students to attend class, Irvin sometimes had difficulty holding their attention. On one occasion class was disrupted when "all were scattered—I may say in an instant—by a drunken Indian who came into the house. Some hid in one place and some [in] another while some went out of the house." On another occasion a classroom full of students "who behaved well" and were "all sober" became "much alarmed from report of a party of Omahas being in march for war against the Ioways and Sacs."[18] By 1841 Irvin and Hamilton claimed fifty students had enrolled in the mission school, though they admitted the average daily attendance was "not more than thirty." In their annual report to the BFM, the missionaries expressed their belief that the Sacs and Foxes would begin to send their children to the school. This optimism was prompted in part by the fact that they had allowed some of their annual annuities to be allocated to the school.[19]

Perhaps buoyed by that optimism, the missionaries began in 1842 to lobby the BFM and the Office of Indian Affairs for funds that would allow them to build a manual training school at the mission. Ioway leaders had told them that they did not like sending their boys away to school because it was difficult to maintain contact with them. No Heart and Raining told Subagent Richardson, "We were formerly opposed to the mission but now we think differently. . . . We think the plan of a boarding school is good. We did send some [children] to [the Kickapoo Academy] but they are now as bad as any of us and we were discouraged but if they are with us all the time it will be better." When Richardson pressed them on the issue of whether they were willing to "give up" their children to the whites that would operate the school, the Ioways replied that they were.[20]

The missionaries offered to build a school on the Ioways' own land. They had convinced the tribe it would be beneficial to teach their children "where their parents and their chiefs can retain the charge of them. [By] keeping their sons thus at home while receiving their education, they hope to guard against their becoming aliens to their own people—a result which unhappily too often follows their remaining for a series of years at a distant school."[21]

Subagent Richardson agreed with the missionaries. In reporting to the Commissioner of Indian Affairs in Washington, Richardson wrote, "If there was a sufficient fund to establish a manual labor school among [the Ioways], I have no doubt it would tend more than anything which would be done for the civilization of these unfortunate people. The Ioways are not averse to having their children educated and instructed in the ways of the whites, but are opposed to sending their children [away] to be educated."[22]

Unlike later government boarding schools that routinely separated Native students from their families, the Presbyterians attempted to educated Ioway children in their own communities. While the close proximity to family and community often provided students with distractions that made it more difficult to keep them in class, the missionaries saw a potentially beneficial trade-off. They hoped that, by educating Ioway children, they might also reach Ioway adults. The General Assembly of the Presbyterian Church of the United States of America (PCUSA) believed that Native parents were "never more likely to be effectually reached and profited than through the medium of their children." Because they were more susceptible to the missionaries' influence, the Presbyterians believed the children

The Ioway, Sac and Fox Mission, 2014. Although the mission could accommodate up to seventy-five students along with the missionaries, workers, and their families, it housed less than half that number during its peak years in the 1850s. (Photograph by Lance Foster.)

could be more easily trained in the ways of civilization. Once adults saw their children toiling happily in the Christian world, they would be far more likely to look favorably upon it themselves.[23]

In their 1844 annual report the missionaries claimed that the Ioways were "extremely anxious" to have the new school built. In August 1843 Ioway headmen had voted to appropriate two thousand dollars of their annuities to the school construction project. As momentum for the project increased, the missionaries optimistically projected that aside from serving the Native population of the Great Nemaha Subagency the school would one day attract "as many children as it could contain." Many of these children, they believed, would come from other Indigenous nations outside of the subagency.[24]

By September 1844 Irvin reported that construction of the new mission school building had finally begun. Half of the two hundred thousand bricks needed for the structure were on-site and "ready to lay up." Seventy acres had been fenced off, ground had been broken, and laborers were employed to lay the foundation and the first story stonework. They expected that pine finish lumber ordered from Pennsylvania for the floors and windows would soon be delivered. The Ioways, Sacs, and Foxes jointly paid for the bulk of the building costs by appropriating $4,675 of their annuities to the project and promising to contribute $1,440 annually to operate the school. The U.S. government contributed an additional $2,000 toward the construction. The missionaries must have viewed the 100-by-36-feet three-story stone-and-brick building as a miraculous improvement over the primitive conditions they had endured for nearly a decade. As it neared completion, they noted "the conditions and prospects of this mission are now more promising than at any former period."[25]

However, widespread illness, inclement weather, and the isolation of the construction site on the subagency delayed the school's completion. In September 1845 the fever (malaria) swept into the subagency. Forty Ioways and twenty Sacs and Foxes died over the winter as a result of the sickness. "Every member of the Mission was attacked," reported the missionaries, "but their lives were mercifully spared." The sickness forced some members of the mission staff to leave. A couple by the name of Coon returned to Pennsylvania and eventually resigned from the mission. Julia Hamilton, William's wife, also returned to Pennsylvania to recuperate with her family. Her husband followed her several months later, leaving the mission shorthanded until they both returned in the fall of 1846.[26]

To compound the misery on the subagency, the winter weather turned exceptionally cold. Workers were able to cover the doorways and install glass in all the windows, but it remained too cold to complete the plasterwork inside the building. The setback meant that the school was not ready in time for classes to begin on April 1, 1846. "The past year has been one of trial for the members of this mission," Irvin and Hamilton wrote in their annual report for that year. We found "the erection of such a building in the midst of the Indian forest to be a very difficult undertaking."[27]

The school finally opened early in the summer 1846. Thirty Ioway students attended the school that year, but the Sacs and Foxes continued to refuse to send their children to the school. This confounded the missionaries, who viewed them as being far more temperate, industrious, and "advanced" than their Ioway neighbors. The Ioways had also "freely" donated money from their annuities to the school. The missionaries speculated that the Sacs and Foxes stayed away from the school because they did not want to associate with the Ioways, though there is no evidence to confirm this was the case. Despite the absence of the Sacs and Foxes, the missionaries reported that "everything is promising in the school; the children are contented."[28]

Not all Ioways were content with the missionaries and their new school, however. Headman Francis White Cloud, who had been in Europe while the school was being built, soon after he returned home asked Subagent William Rucker to replace Irvin and Hamilton. He complained that, though the missionaries had been with the Ioways a decade, they had been of no help to them. White Cloud also charged the missionaries with inflating the number of students attending the school in order to make their mission appear more successful than it was. He alleged that when Thomas Harvey, Superintendent of Indian Affairs in St. Louis, visited the subagency in the fall of 1846, the missionaries collected "a great many" children, clothed them and took them to the school in order to "make a show to the superintendent." As soon as Harvey left, White Cloud claimed, the missionaries took back the clothing and "sent [the children] home naked." White Cloud said that only ten children regularly attended the school, though he believed more Ioway children would stay at the school if the missionaries fed them better. "The reason the children . . . don't like to stay is that they . . . do not get enough to eat."[29]

White Cloud also charged the missionaries with misappropriating seven hundred dollars from the Ioways' annuities to buy clothing and supplies for the children. During Harvey's visit in 1846 he asked the superintendent how the missionaries were able to make withdrawals from the fund without the Ioways' permission. When Harvey made no attempt to answer his question, White Cloud persisted. He told the superintendent the money could have been used to buy flour, sugar, and coffee. Harvey answered dismissively that he did not believe the Ioways would know what to do with flour, sugar, and coffee.[30]

Despite White Cloud's opposition, the school remained open. The large new building, which never operated at more than half the capacity for which it was designed, allowed the missionaries to devote space for specific religious and educational tasks. The ground floor included a dining room, kitchen, pantry, milk house, and two sleeping rooms. The second

The White Cloud, Head Chief of the Iowas, 1844/1845 (oil on canvas). George Catlin (1796–1872). Francis White Cloud was the son of MaxúThka (White Cloud), an Ioway leader who became a strong ally of the United States in his later years. While the younger White Cloud respected his father's views, he was unable to forgive the United States for the way its government had treated his people. (Paul Mellon Collection, National Gallery of Art.)

floor contained a chapel, boys' and girls' sleeping rooms, and private quarters used by Hamilton and Irvin and their families. On the third floor were more sleeping rooms for students, a private quarter for a female teacher, and a study used by Irvin. "The building," wrote Irvin "promises to be a great blessing to these Indians, as well as the destitute tribes in their vicinity."[31]

By September 1850 Hamilton reported that thirty-eight students were enrolled in the school. The average daily attendance that year was thirty-five students. These figures would not change significantly over the next decade. Although nearly half the students who attended the school that year were of mixed heritage, the missionaries identified the majority as Ioways. They indicated that they had finally admitted a small number of Sac and Fox children and listed the remaining students as being members of the Sioux, Otoe, and Blackfeet Nations. Twenty-three were boys and fifteen were girls. Later Irvin commented that the school might be called the "Orphan Asylum," as nearly all of the children who attended it had lost their parents. Roughly half the students could read, either in English or in the Ioways' language.[32]

Ioway students at the mission school were allowed to maintain close contact with their families and their communities, but the missionaries subjected all students to some of the same methods of cultural assimilation that would be used in federal boarding schools later in the nineteenth century. Irvin and Hamilton forced children to give up their own clothing. The students were required to wear donated clothing that the mission had received from the BFM. It appears that the clothing varied and availability of certain items depended entirely on what the BFM home office was able to provide. On at least one occasion the missionaries wrote to the board to complain that the clothes they received were the wrong size. In 1851 they reported that clothing included in a recent shipment had been large enough to fit grown men and was of little use to the younger boys at the school.[33]

The missionaries also routinely assigned Christian names to new students. In some instances the BFM in Pittsburg sent specific names of benefactors to the missionaries so that they might be given to children. In 1854, for example, the missionaries received a letter from BFM secretary Walter Lowrie stating that a patron had requested that one of the mission scholars be named David Crowell. "Tell the good lady who gave you the money that we think [the child who received that name] is just such a boy as she would be pleased with," reported Irvin, "broad full face, bright eyes, healthy and smart, about 5 years of age, from the Shian [Cheyenne] tribe." Earlier the missionaries had written to Lowrie asking if he wanted them to send descriptions of new scholars to the home office so names could be assigned there. Or, they asked, would it be better for the BFM to send the mission a list of names for new scholars to receive upon entering the school. Irvin and Hamilton also assigned names to the children when none had been provided by the BFM. "Several," they reported, "were named for clergymen."[34]

The missionaries subjected the students at the mission school to a highly structured daily routine, which Irvin described in 1853. The children rose at five o'clock each morning and were washed, combed, and ready for chapel by six. The older girls took turns preparing breakfast while the rest of the children attended chapel and then moved on to the dining room where everyone ate together. After breakfast all girls except those helping in the kitchen worked on sewing and knitting until a quarter to nine. During that same time the boys did chores on the mission farm. This practical work was considered an important part of the children's education. Lowrie, the driving force behind many of the BFM's programs, believed it was crucial that students receive a practical education in farming and in the "mechanical arts."[35]

At nine o'clock the school day began. Students studied until four in the afternoon, taking time for morning recess, afternoon recess, and an hour-long lunch break. After school the girls returned to their sewing and the boys to the farm until half past five, when they all ate supper. Immediately after the evening meal there was worship in the dining hall. From seven until eight the children separated once more by gender for singing, exercise, and prayers until bedtime.[36]

During school hours the children studied from some of the same books that their white counterparts used in schools across the country. They read from Panley's *Geography*, McGuffy's *Readers*, and Cobb's *Readers*. Because religious training was an integral part of the Presbyterians' educational plan, the missionaries spent a great deal of time teaching the students scripture, psalms, and hymns. On Sundays the students were subjected to Bible class and a sermon in the morning, classes in the afternoon, and a lecture in the evening. Students learned to read the Testaments and memorized portions of Brown's *Catechism*. The missionaries rewarded students who could recite all of the Presbyterians' *Shorter Catechism* perfectly with a Bible. The missionaries printed hymnals and texts in the Ioways' language for use in church, but they used English texts in the classroom and requested donations of books from their Presbyterian patrons to give to students as rewards for good behavior and academic achievement.[37]

Student retention proved to be a chronic problem for the missionaries. While there were a variety of reasons for this, many children left because their families moved away. In 1851 the school lost four students, including William White Cloud and Charles White Crow, when Francis White Cloud's band of Ioways moved fifteen miles away to live north of the Great Nemaha River on the Half-Breed Reservation. Fanny Lee was taken by her mother to live among the Otoes in present-day Nebraska. The following year Raining's son Lewis left the school after his father died and Sylvania Robidioux left to be with her mother who had also moved to the Half-Breed Reservation. The missionaries admitted that even the orphans often left because they felt the pull of their extended family. "Their domestic regulations are different from ours," wrote Irvin. "The control of a remote relation is at times as absolute as that of the parent."[38]

Irvin and Hamilton also had to contend with those students who ran away from the school. In the fall of 1851 the missionaries reported that several of the smaller boys in the school repeatedly tried to run away. One of those boys may have been William Campbell, who made frequent attempts to run away during the months that followed. Hamilton described Campbell as a small and smart boy who seemed "determined to have his own way."[39]

Children often ran away from the school in order to be reunited with their families. Joseph Banks was the son of William Banks, a Holt County, Missouri, farmer who also operated a store and hemp warehouse at Iowa Point, and an Ioway woman named Waru'skami (Giant Woman). After Joseph's mother died his father sent him to the mission school. One day, in August 1858, as Banks and some acquaintances sat on the warehouse platform in Iowa Point, they observed Joseph and four other Native boys coming from the direction of the school. "Them boys have run away, I'll bet," Banks told his companions. Soon, the Reverend Irvin arrived on horseback to take the boys back to the mission. As Irvin prepared to leave with the boys, William Banks informed him that Joseph would not be

returning with him. Joseph stayed with his father and did not return to
the mission.[40] In his 1847 *Annual Report*, Irvin reflected:

> It is a great drawback to the benefit of the scholars, that they are so
> soon taken from the school to assist their parents, or that they should
> yield to the solicitations of their companions and leave it of their own
> accord. Their places, it is true, are supplied by younger children, but
> the full advantage of a religious training is only partially effected,
> on account of their irregular attendance, and the success of tempta-
> tions to leave the school entirely at an early age.[41]

Occasionally, students were so troublesome that the missionaries sent
them away. One Ioway boy who caused a great deal of trouble at the mission school was Francis Dupee, who was about twelve years of age in 1851,
an inquisitive boy who once surprised Irvin by quizzing him outside of
class about the meaning of some of his religious lessons. He asked Irvin
what Christ meant when he said "follow me and I will make you fishers of
men" and asked him why Peter told Christ "repent for me for I am a sinful man." In the fall of 1851 Dupee talked a Sac boy into helping him burn
down the mission barn. After starting the fire the boys ran off, but Dupee's father soon returned his son to the mission to be punished. The missionaries did not want Dupee to remain at the school where he might cause
more trouble for them, and they felt he was too smart to be turned out to
live among the "wild Indians." With his father's consent, they decided to send
him to St. Louis to "put him to a trade."[42]

One Ioway student whom the missionaries deemed a success was Kirwin Murray. Raised at the mission, Murray worked on the Sac and Fox
farm as a boy and helped the missionaries at the Otoe and Omaha Mission
when he grew a bit older. In 1855 he married a Native woman who had
also grown up at the mission. Great Nemaha Agent Daniel Vanderslice
spoke highly of the young couple saying "the highly respectable manner
in which they live is highly credible to them." He added they were a "salu-
tary influence on the students at the school and on the . . . tribe to which
they belonged." After the sudden death of John B. Roy in November 1859,
Vanderslice hired Murray to replace him as the Ioways' interpreter. Later
Murray would be one of forty-four Ioways to serve in the Union Army
during the Civil War. In the late 1870s he was among a group of Ioways

Kirwin Murray, ca. 1880. Kirwin Murray was one of the few Ioways that Presbyterian missionaries Samuel Irvin and William Hamilton considered to have succeeded in the mission school. Murray went on to be a Civil War soldier and a leader among the Ioways who traveled south to the Indian Territory in the 1870s and 1880s. (Friends Historical Library of Swarthmore College.)

who chose to leave the Great Nemaha Agency and resettle in the Indian Territory, now known as Oklahoma. In 1894 Murray served as an interpreter to a delegation of Ioways who visited Washington.[43]

Despite their relative lack of success with the Ioways and their inability to engage in any meaningful way with the Sacs and Foxes, Irvin and Hamilton set their sights on expanding their mission. At about the same time as the mission school opened in 1846, the BFM established a new mission among the Otoes and Omahas near the site of present-day Bellevue, Nebraska. Although the Presbyterians assigned Edward McKinney to oversee the mission, Hamilton spent several months assisting there and was transferred to the site permanently in 1854. In the beginning Hamilton and Irvin hoped the Otoe and Omaha Mission would provide them with students for the Ioway, Sac and Fox Mission School. "Some of the Omahas and Otoes desire to have their children admitted to this school," the missionaries pointed out soon after the new mission opened. Irvin argued that bringing students from outlying nations to the mission school on the Great Nemaha Agency would be a cost savings for the government. He added that it would be safer for the children, who were less likely to be stolen by family or killed by "marauding bands of wild" Indians. Although students from other nations did attend the school, they tended to be children without families to care for them and never attended in numbers that matched the hopes of Irvin and Hamilton.[44]

The fortunes of the Ioway, Sac and Fox Mission changed for the worse in the early 1850s, as political momentum for the creation of the Kansas Territory began. Suddenly Irvin found himself in the defensive position, having to justify the existence of the school and the mission. As early as 1852 Irvin wrote to the BFM to inform them that the "knowing ones" in the region were of the opinion that the organization of the new territory would include a treaty to open at least half of the Great Nemaha Agency to white settlement. At that time Irvin believed the new, smaller agency would be situated between the mission and the Missouri River. This made sense, as it would have left the mission, the agency buildings, and most of the improvements the government had made still within the agency boundaries.

By early 1853, however, some settlers were lobbying for the Ioways, Sacs, and Foxes to be removed from the territory altogether. The missionaries touted the benefits of allowing them to remain where they were and argued that their mission was one of the main reasons for doing so. If the Natives and the mission school were allowed to stay, the missionaries reasoned, Ioway students would enjoy the benefits that incoming settlers would bring to the area, while still being surrounded by their school, their families, and their culture. As preparations for the formation of the territory and new treaties with the Ioways, Sacs, and Foxes progressed, the missionaries skillfully linked their efforts to save their mission with a campaign to allow the Natives to retain their homes on the Great Nemaha Agency. "If we don't attend to our own interests and that of the Indians, we may be sure [those who want the Ioways' land] will not attend to them for us," Irvin declared.[45]

In the months immediately preceding the treaty negotiations it began to look as though the Ioways, Sacs, and Foxes would be moved a few miles north, away from the mission. Part of the reasoning behind this was to keep them away from the heavily used branch of the Oregon Trail that passed just north of the mission school building. Walter Lowrie informed Irvin that, if they moved the agency, the BFM was inclined to continue operating the school at its present location, even though it would be ten or twelve miles away from the Ioways' new settlements. "This plan will not be without its difficulties," Irvin replied, "but seeing there are so [many] improvements made and the school is started, it is perhaps the least that you can do."[46]

On May 17, 1854, the Ioways signed a treaty that greatly reduced the size of their agency and forced them to move their settlements north, closer to the Great Nemaha River. The Sacs and Foxes signed a similar treaty the following day. Six months later most of the Ioways had moved to their new homes, and plans were underway to survey the land surrounding the mission for white settlement. Just months after the move, Agent Vanderslice reported that many of the Ioways who previously had supported the mission school no longer wanted to send their children there. While this may have been due in part to the distance between the Ioways' new homes and the mission, it was also because the Ioways were uncomfortable with the number of children from other tribes who attended.

In the years following the Treaty of 1854, the attendance at the mission school remained static. "For some time past, we had been a great deal encouraged about the Iowa[y]s sending more children," Irvin reported to Lowrie nearly five years after the move. "But the scale has turned. They have taken away some that were here and raised old objections," about the school being too expensive and too far away.[47] In 1859 Irvin reported that, of the forty-four students enrolled in the mission school, nearly half were Sioux, and many of those were orphans. Traders who dealt regularly with the Sioux told him there were many more orphans from that tribe who would be willing to attend the school or one like it. At the same time an Ioway man told Irvin that many Ioways would also like to send their children to the school but did not want Ioways attending with the children of their old enemies. "But let the Iowa[y]s take what course they may," an exasperated Irvin wrote to Lowrie. "Has not the board waited on [them] long enough?" He pointed out that for two decades the missionaries had offered the Gospels to the Ioways, and they had tried to persuade them to attend the mission school for a dozen years. If the Ioways were unwilling to accept the BFM's offer, the missionaries believed, others would.[48]

Even as Irvin wrote those words, however, the Bureau of Indian Affairs was preparing to write the mission school out of their plans for the Ioways' future. In 1859 Agent Vanderslice met with Commissioner of Indian Affairs Albert Greenwood in Washington to discuss replacing the mission school with a day school that would be built closer to the site of the new agency buildings. At the same time Vanderslice also requested that the Methodists send a missionary to live among the Ioways. In September of that year Irvin had an opportunity to discuss this turn of events face-to-face with Commissioner Greenwood. The commissioner told the missionary that the bureau was not likely to renew the contract they had with the BFM to operate either the Otoe or the Ioway mission school. Greenwood pointed out that the Ioways got very little in return for the money they spent on the school, and he believed day schools near the Ioways' and Otoes' agencies would be a more efficient educational tool.[49]

Meanwhile enrollment at the Ioway, Sac and Fox Mission School continued to decline. Irvin hoped to prop up his sagging attendance figures with students from outside the agency, but he was unable to do so. In April 1860 Irvin sent a list of students to Lowrie. Of the twenty students enrolled in the school, only four—Eliza Noheart, Lizza Cruthers, Mary Childs, and Sophia Campbell—were identified as Ioways. Of the others, eleven were Sioux, four were Blackfeet, and one was Pawnee.[50] After twenty-three years at the Great Nemaha Agency, the Presbyterians were forced to accept that they had failed in their mission to bring the salvation of Christ and a common education to the Ioways, Sacs, and Foxes. The mission continued to struggle a few years longer, but its fate was finally sealed when the Civil War broke out in the spring of 1861. This forced the BFM to scale back many of its missions across the United States. The Ioway, Sac and Fox Mission closed its doors in 1863. The building served as an orphanage for Native children until 1866, when it was closed altogether. Neither Samuel Irvin nor William Hamilton returned to Pennsylvania. Irvin remained in the vicinity of his former mission and founded an academy in the nearby town of Highland, Kansas. Hamilton spent the rest of his life in Nebraska, not far from the old Otoe and Omaha Mission site.

The Ioway, Sac and Fox Mission School failed for a number of reasons. Teacher retention and adequate funding were a constant problem for the missionaries. In retrospect, however, it is evident the school failed largely because the Presbyterians naively believed the Ioways, Sacs, and Foxes would willingly embrace Christianity once they were exposed to it. The atmosphere in which Irvin and Hamilton taught Ioway children was far different from that which would define the federal-boarding-school system for Indian children in the late nineteenth and early twentieth centuries. In federal boarding schools the government dictated the terms by which Native children were educated. By removing students from their families and often their communities, federal officials found they were able to exert control over the students' daily lives by dictating how they dressed, how they behaved, and which language they spoke. These restrictions, officials believed, led to a higher success rate for acculturating the children into mainstream society.

By comparison, Irvin and Hamilton's control over students who attended the Ioway, Sac and Fox Mission School was compromised by its location on the reservation and by the students' ability to maintain contact with their families and culture. Regular attendance was a constant problem that vexed the missionaries. In writing about Dakota children and the missionaries who attempted to educate them in the 1840s and 1850s, Linda Clemmons has observed that the Dakota children like the Ioways were voluntary boarders, educated near their villages and families, so these missionary educational "programs were two-way encounters based on negotiation and compromise." The missionaries exerted a great deal of influence and control over the children while they were in the mission building, but the children's families dictated the terms by which their offspring attended the schools. "Because parents chose to send their children to live with the missionaries, and could take them away at any time," Clemmons argues, "they had the ability to negotiate the terms of their children's education."[51] So it was with the Ioways.

Many Ioways showed resistance to European American education, but at least some—most notably the headman No Heart—supported the construction of the mission school on the subagency and agreed to appropriate a significant amount of money toward its completion. "Our children know enough Indian already," No Heart declared. "We wish them to learn English and become White men." In the 1844 report to the BFM, the missionaries quoted an Ioway leader, whom they did not identify, as saying, "Many of us feel inclined to change our way of living, and are anxious to see our children raised up to business, and habits of virtue." The missionaries' implication was that at least some Ioways wanted their children to learn to live as the whites lived.[52]

David Wallace Adams has outlined three common reasons that Native leaders consented to send their children to white schools. First, he contends they often did so because they believed this was the only way Native people could learn the skills they needed to survive in a white world. After years of treaty negotiations, tribal leaders often came to believe that a white education was their only defense in trying to protect their land and culture. Second, Adams argues that Native children sometimes attended school in order to escape the poverty and desperation of their villages. Finally, Native leaders often agreed to send their children to schools simply because it was the better of what they perceived to be two options— extermination or extinction.[53]

Certainly the Ioways weighed those same options during their early years on the subagency. Many in the tribe were old enough to have witnessed the forty-year trail of decimation that had pushed them to the west bank of the Missouri River. They had seen typhoid and cholera shrink their numbers from nearly one thousand in 1837 to less than half of that a decade later. Increased contact with settlers made the Ioways more aware of the power of the U.S. government and more conscious of their own poverty. If the headmen were charged with ensuring the Ioways' survival, it is understandable that some, like No Heart, believed acculturation seemed a necessary price to pay for that survival.[54] Still, traditions die hard and like many Native peoples, the Ioways, Sacs, and Foxes held firm to the old ways, tolerating the Presbyterians rather than accepting the message they carried.

CHAPTER 4

A Change in Ioway Leadership

The traditional model of Ioway leadership, which was based on balance and the decentralization of authority and power, stood in stark contrast to European forms of government and social hierarchy. The Ioways based part of their style of government on their oral traditions, according to which the ancestors of the Earth clans and Sky clans come together to form the Ioway nation. The Bear nation, which came from a world below the earth, led the Beaver, Elk, and Eagle clans. The Buffalo nation, which led the Owl, Pigeon, and Snake clans, came from a place in the sky. Walking the earth, the people found that life was hard. The two groups met and shared their sacred pipes. During their conversation they decided that it would be beneficial to both Sky and Earth clans if they came together to become one people.[1]

Following the steps of those old ones and in the spirit of cooperation they displayed, members of those two clans shared equal responsibility for leading the Ioways. Each fall the sound of the elk's mating whistle signaled it was time for the Bear clan to govern the people. They led throughout the fall and winter, as that was the time of year the Bear ancestors first emerged upon the earth. At the first sound of the small green tree frogs in the spring, the Buffalo clan assumed the responsibility of tribal leadership.

Even the arrangement of the village reflected the balance of power between the Sky and Earth clans. The Ioways divided their camp circle into two halves; the lodges of the Sky clans occupied one side while the lodges of the Earth clans occupied the other.[2] The leaders of the Ioway people camped in the center of the circle. In their civic government the Ioways considered the leader of either the Bear or the Buffalo clan chiefs to be their principal headman during the six months that his clan governed the tribe. This leader was not the supreme ruler of his people. He led with the help of a council, and his decisions were not considered final until the council reached consensus. The oldest living male descendants of the eldest of the original male clan ancestors held positions on the council. If a clan leader had no sons to inherit his position, the son of a daughter or the son of a niece could succeed him upon the leader's death.[3]

A separate set of headmen led the military affairs of the nation. These were the keepers of the various clans' war bundles. A warrior who wanted to raise a war party consulted the bundle keepers first. The keepers opened the war bundles and sang appropriate songs in ceremony to determine whether to allow the warrior to go to war. Once this was affirmed and a war party selected, the bundle keepers oversaw the preparation for battle with several days of fasting, sweat lodges, and other rites of purification. This process ensured that a warrior desired to fight for the good of the people, not for personal glory, and that battles were executed in a way that conformed to the Ioways' sense of morality and spirituality.[4]

This well-designed balance of power, which stood for centuries, slowly dissolved as the nation came into contact with white traders, European colonial officials, and U.S. Indian agents. The Ioways' first experience with European concepts of power came in the wake of their commercial contact with the French in the 1670s. By the 1680s they were heavily involved in selling furs to traders operating out of the Green Bay. As business increased throughout the eighteenth and nineteenth centuries, non-Native traders became a regular presence in Ioway villages. Not surprisingly, some traders took Ioway women to be their "country wives" despite having wives at home. For example, Joseph Robidoux, the founder of St. Joseph, Missouri, had children with an Ioway woman while his "town wife," Angelique, lived in St. Louis with the couple's seven children.[5]

"Country" marriages were one outcome of non-Native men working and living among the tribes with whom they traded. Often these marriages brought wealth and business opportunities that upset the traditional balance of leadership among the Ioways. Martha Royce Blaine reports that in traditional times, marriage among the Ioways was dictated by a strict class system. The children of headmen married one another, as did the offspring of war leaders and those of common people. A man who wanted to marry an Ioway woman brought her parents gifts such as ponies, blankets, and clothing, the amount and value of the gifts dictated by her class.[6]

Traders, however, could choose a wife from any class and offer gifts that might or might not be commensurate with the social standing of the bride's family. The husband-to-be and a representative of the potential wife's family negotiated the terms. In 1849 an Ioway woman unsuccessfully attempted to arrange a marriage between her thirteen-year-old daughter, Anenein, and the Swiss artist Rudolph Friedrich Kurz. The woman asked Kurz for a pony and a wool blanket. She requested "good food" and an outfit of new clothes for the girl and seventy pounds of ground meal for the rest of the family. She also asked Kurz to promise that he would not beat the girl. When farmer and trader William Banks married the nineteen-year-old Ioway widow Waru'skami in 1844, he gave her family a pony, blankets, cloth, and other items.[7]

While such arrangements brought Ioway families goods they needed and, sometimes, luxuries they could not otherwise afford, marriages between Ioway women and non-Native men could also provide Ioways with lucrative business opportunities. For example, an Ioway leader whom Kurz called Kirusche promised to reward the artist with two thousand acres of land if he would marry the headman's daughter, Witthae, and live with her family. In addition, however, Kirusche wanted Kurz to enter into a business partnership with him. Kirusche needed Kurz's help to purchase and operate a stone quarry that he believed might help him make enough money to support his extended family.[8]

Like marriage negotiations between European nobility, marriages between traders and Ioway women often came with opportunities for both sides. A trader could count on having an exclusive business relationship with his bride's family, and members of that family often gained prestige in their village because of their direct access to the trader's goods. Joseph Robidoux's trade relationship with the Ioways was enhanced when his Ioway daughter, Mary, became the wife of Ioway headman Francis White Cloud.[9]

Exclusive trade and business relationships sometimes elevated the power of Ioway men who did not have the hereditary right to become headmen.

Individuals who accumulated wealth through trade networks gained the ability, previously held exclusively by hereditary leaders, to determine how the goods were distributed throughout the nation. This not only led to divisive jealousies and rivalries, it upset the delicate balance of power that centuries of tradition had been able to maintain.[10]

A similar disruption in tradition occurred after the Ioways began to interact with the representatives of European governments. As the colonial powers of France, Spain, and England entered the Missouri River valley, they began to cultivate diplomatic relationships with Ioway leaders. Unaccustomed to the time-consuming process of dealing with a council instead of one ruler, European colonists often selected one leader with whom they were willing to do business, and bestowed honorary titles and gifts upon him. Such was the case in 1776 when seven Ioway headmen and their families traveled to Montreal with a delegation of Dakotas, Winnebagos, Sacs, and Foxes to meet with Frederick Haldimand, governor and chief of the British provinces. On behalf of King George III, Haldimand awarded certain headmen, including the Ioway Wamúnu (The Thief) with medals of friendship and peace.[11] Like trade goods, European gifts such as flags, certificates, and medals had the potential to greatly enhance the prestige of Ioway leaders among their own people. Native leaders were especially fond of engraved peace medals. For those who received them these medals were not only mementos of a council or meeting with a foreign leader, they became emblems of power and stature. Ioway headmen had long worn bear claw necklaces to symbolize their spiritual and social leadership status within the tribe. Ioway leaders earned the right to wear these necklaces through means that were tied to tradition. Medals, on the other hand, came from outside the nation and were given for reasons that had nothing to do with Ioway customs. Therefore, it was possible for someone who was not recognized as a leader among the Ioways to receive a medal from a European power. Often the mere possession of this rare artifact could elevate the recipient to a position previously held only by a traditional headman. This too created jealousy within the tribe and disrupted traditions of Ioway leadership.[12]

In 1809 the United States took this disruption one step further. Government leaders sought to influence Ioway politics directly by selecting a single headman to be the lone authority with whom they could negotiate treaties and agreements. President Thomas Jefferson presented

Wayín̄Wèxa (Hard Heart) with documents and a medal that identified him as the "Head Chief "of all the Ioway people. As the concept of a single leader ran counter to the Ioways' traditional balance of powers, Jefferson's designation elevated Hard Heart to a level of authority that no previous leader had enjoyed. Hard Heart proved to be a reliable backer of the United States, which eventually split the tribe. He persuaded a "formidable number" of Ioways not to side with the British during the War of 1812 and led them to the west side of the Missouri River, away from the conflict, where they lived for a time with their relatives, the Otoes.[13]

In the summer of 1823 Hard Heart died while fighting with a group of Yankton Dakotas. The U.S. government chose White Cloud to follow him as the head chief of the Ioways.[14] At nearly forty years of age, White Cloud supported the United States and its effort to reform Indian people, but that road had been a long one. He was a veteran of eighteen battles with Ioway enemies and had once been tried for the murder of two French traders. At a peace council in 1819 he had boldly contradicted Benjamin O'Fallon, the Indian Agent of the Missouri River, to warn him that the United States had no business meddling in disputes between rival tribes. Four years later at the time of Hard Heart's death, however, his attitude toward the United States was more pragmatic.[15] He understood that resisting white settlement was no longer a viable option for the Ioway people, and he supported the government's efforts to train the Indigenous people of the lower Missouri River valley to live, farm, and govern themselves in the same way that the white people did.

This realization had led White Cloud, along with the Ioway headman Great Walker, to sell the northern half of Missouri to the U.S. government for five thousand dollars in 1824; the first-ever cession of Ioway tribal land. Six years later, at a large treaty council at Prairie du Chien, White Cloud expressed his desire to work cooperatively with the United States. Waving his war club in the air, he declared, "When I was young, I used to pride myself in one of these things, but now I mean to throw it aside. I know of other things."[16]

In 1834 White Cloud's cooperation with the U.S. government led to his murder. Three years earlier, a group of Omahas had killed the son of the Ioway headman Crane. As he had in previous cases of intertribal violence, White Cloud felt it was the responsibility of the U.S. military to bring justice to those who committed the murder. When a dozen Ioway men

launched a retaliatory raid and killed six Omaha men, taking a woman
and a child hostage, White Cloud assisted Ioway Subagent Hughes in cap-
turing eight of the Ioways believed to be responsible. While in jail in Fort
Leavenworth, one of the imprisoned Ioways threatened to kill White Cloud
for assisting in his arrest. In 1834 after making his escape from the fort,
the man raised a party to track White Cloud down. The party followed
the leader up the Nodaway River; they caught and killed him in the vicinity
of present-day Montgomery County, Iowa.[17]

    In death White Cloud quickly achieved mythic stature as one of the last
of a generation of Ioway who remembered a time when the tribe had lived
according to their traditional ways. While he had been forced to give up
many of those ways, Native and white people alike held him up as an icon
symbolizing their virtues. At the same time many believed that he symbolized the ability of Native people to work closely with the U.S. government in their efforts to reform them.[18]

    White Cloud's death thrust his young son Francis into a position of lead-
ership. Roughly twenty-three years old at the time, the younger White
Cloud acknowledged that he was unprepared to assume the role of headman and refused to accept the position without the consensus of his fellow
Ioways. According to Commissioner of Indian Affairs Thomas McKenney,
who interviewed Francis White Cloud in 1837, he asked that a general
council of the nation convene to establish whether the Ioways wanted
him to serve as a headman. Both the tribe and its elders decided that he
should accept the role. Francis White Cloud agreed but then asked his
father's brother No Heart to act as his guide and mentor. Then in his late
thirties No Heart had been a successful warrior—participating in war
parties against the Dakota Sioux, Osages, and Pawnees with his brother
the elder White Cloud and his father, MáHége (Wounding Arrow). In recent years he had worked to end the conflict with the Omahas that had
played a part in his brother's death. Thomas McKenney also interviewed
No Heart in 1837 and reported the Ioway leader was "inclined to peace
and has been friendly towards the whites."[19]

    For a time, No Heart's role as Ioway headman eclipsed that of his
nephew. Beginning in late 1834, the Ioways elected to have the elder leader
receive the annuities that the U.S. government paid them as part of the
Treaty of 1824. This gave No Heart the opportunity to play the traditional
role of a headman by distributing the annuities to his people.[20] A council

Na'hjeNing'e (No Heart) was White Cloud's younger brother. When his
nephew Francis White Cloud became the Ioways' headman at a young
age, No Heart served as his advisor. Less combative and mercurial than
his nephew, No Heart was a stabilizing force for the Ioways, as well as a
consistent supporter of the U.S. government. (The State Historical Society
of Missouri.)

of leaders supported No Heart and White Cloud in decision-making. Among those who signed treaties and attended councils during that period were Waích^eMáñi (War Leader; the whites often referred to him as the Orator), ÑíyuMáñi (Raining), and Wadwá^n (Pumpkin).

As he eased into the role of Ioway headman, the younger White Cloud declared that he would follow in his father's footsteps to lead his people toward assimilation. Like his father Francis spoke of the benefits of living in peace and of learning to adopt a Euro-American lifestyle. "One of my sisters and other young [Ioway women] have been taught to spin and weave," he told McKenney. "My father approved of this and encouraged it. He also taught the lessons of peace, and counseled me not to go to war, except in my own defense." He set an example for other Ioways by farming sixteen acres of land, the produce from which he distributed to those of his people who were in need.[21]

But even before he assumed the mantle of leadership, Francis White Cloud was troubled by resentments that made it difficult for him to lead his people blindly toward assimilation. He was angry over the U.S. government's failure to keep its promise and prevent settlers from illegally squatting in the Platte country west of Missouri's original border, land set aside for the Ioways, Sacs, Foxes, and several other tribes to share as part of the Treaty of 1824. Almost as soon as the Ioways, Sacs, and Foxes had moved out of the state to their new agency on the Platte River, settlers had followed. This sometimes led to trouble, as it did in 1829 when citizens from Missouri crossed into Indian land and stole horses and other personal property from White Cloud's own family. Frustrated by the U.S. military's inability to prevent such incidents or to bring the perpetrators to justice, White Cloud's father had reacted by physically lashing out against the Ioway Agency's farmer Mr. Bangs.[22]

Andrew Hughes, government agent at the Ioway Agency, which also included the Sacs and Foxes of the Missouri, received reports of settlers living so close to Ioway villages that their cattle were destroying fields of corn. A Sac and Fox leader told Hughes's supervisor John Dougherty, "Bad White men rob us of our horses, guns, blankets, money, hoes and axes, in short everything except our corn . . . we are too proud to go about begging, and we are too weak to steal."[23]

The effort to find a long-term solution to this problem provided Francis White Cloud with one of his first great challenges as a leader. He was forced to contend with the fact that, even when his people attempted to assimilate, their white neighbors refused accept them. The settlers, it seemed, would not be happy until they owned all of the land between Missouri's original western border and the Missouri River. White Cloud, along with the other Ioway, Sac, and Fox leaders began to favor the idea of giving up their land for a new home west of the Missouri River. They hoped that the river would act as a natural buffer between them and the settlers and that in a new land they could go on with their lives without interference from land-hungry settlers.

At Fort Leavenworth, on September 17, 1836, Francis White Cloud, No Heart, and ten other Ioway headmen, along with sixteen Sac and Fox leaders signed a treaty commonly known as the Platte Purchase. The agreement made the Platte River country a part of the state of Missouri. In return, the Ioways, Sacs, and Foxes received four hundred square miles west of the Missouri River. White Cloud seems to have played a large part in the negotiations leading up to the treaty. On paper he was the first of the twelve Ioway headmen present that day to sign the agreement. In the collective memory of Ioways and whites alike, he remains to this day the Ioway leader most associated with the agreement.

One enduring piece of folklore tells of Francis White Cloud sitting in a secluded place on a bluff overlooking the Missouri River in the days before he signed the Platte Purchase. In that spot he prayed for guidance in the matter of the treaty and asked Ma^un, the Creator, to guide him to the best solution for his people. While he prayed White Cloud noticed a plant called plantain growing around him on the bluff top. Plantain was commonly known as white man's foot, because it was an invasive plant transplanted from Europe that seemed to precede white settlers as they migrated across the continent. Noting the arrival of white man's foot on the bluff, White Cloud is said to have realized that there was nothing the Ioways could do to stop the encroachment of the whites. It was at this moment, legend has it, that he decided to sign the treaty. While the historical accuracy of this legend is dubious, it portrays White Cloud as the deciding force behind the passage of the agreement and the decision to move west.[24]

White Cloud seems to have been less involved in the resolution of a land dispute the Ioways had with the Sacs and Foxes of the Mississippi a few months later. In December 1836 six Ioway headmen sat down with Andrew Hughes to draft a petition to Congress and to President Andrew

Jackson. In the petition the Ioways stated that they still held claim to land in eastern Iowa and that they opposed the so-called Mississippi branch of the Sacs' and Foxes' attempts to cede that land to the United States without Ioway approval. Although the petition lists Francis White Cloud as the "1st Chief of the [Ioway] Nation," neither he nor No Heart signed the document. The Orator, Raining, and four other Ioways signed the petition, but No Heart seems to have led the effort to rectify the Ioways' grievance.

It is unclear whether White Cloud even made the trip to Washington, D.C., in the fall of 1837 to meet with the Commissioner of Indian Affairs about the land issue. His name does not appear on the treaty document. In those meetings it was No Heart who took the lead in the negotiations and who produced his famous map to help bolster the Ioways' land claim against the Sacs and Foxes of the Mississippi. And it was No Heart—along with Raining, the Orator, and one other Ioway headman—who signed the final agreement with the United States in November 1837.[25]

While noteworthy, White Cloud's apparent absence from the 1837 treaty and the negotiations that preceded it may simply have been because he was engaged in leading his people to their new subagency west of the Missouri River. The move and the Ioways' new life on a confined land reserve would test the skills of No Heart and White Cloud in the coming years. It also proved to highlight the differences between the two leaders. No Heart, who was once described as the "principal business man of the nation" and its "chief speaker," became the consistent leader who could reliably be counted on to support the agenda of the white missionaries and government agents. White Cloud, whom whites generally characterized as being mercurial, uncooperative, and intemperate, evolved into a voice of opposition and resistance against white intervention into the Ioways' way of life.[26]

The move across the Missouri River in the spring of 1837 was surely a huge undertaking, given the logistics involved in relocating 992 Ioways and 510 Sacs and Foxes. The U.S. government had pledged to ease their transition by providing the nations with cash assistance (five hundred dollars for the Ioways and four hundred dollars for the Sacs and Foxes) and a year's rations. White Cloud, No Heart, and other Ioway leaders became frustrated with the government's failure to follow through with their promises in a timely manner.[27] Nearly a year after their move, Agent Dougherty, who oversaw the new Great Nemaha Subagency and its subagent, reminded

Superintendent of Indian Affairs William Clark that the Ioways, Sacs, and Foxes had yet to receive their cash assistance or rations. Dougherty informed Clark that the residents of the new subagency were "very much dissatisfied with the government [and that] all confidence in it and its officers [was] totally destroyed."[28]

Even before moving to the subagency, White Cloud was unhappy with the manner in which the U.S. government planned to distribute annuities. He wanted the cash delivered directly to him so that he could determine how the goods and money would be distributed throughout the tribe. In traditional Ioway society, the ability to deliver goods and food to the people and to ensure they did not lack for necessities was the sign of a great leader. After moving the Ioways to the subagency, the government sought to bypass the headmen and distribute annuities directly to individual Ioways. White Cloud believed that his peoples' reliance on the government for nearly all their food and clothing was degrading. To be denied the opportunity to decide how those goods and the tribe annuities would be allocated only added to his humiliation. This initiated what would be a long-running dispute between White Cloud and several Great Nemaha subagents.

The power of the subagents to control such transactions had been enhanced by the Intercourse Act of 1834. The law gave Indian agents and their regional supervisors the power to license traders. Its stated purpose—to give local employees of the Bureau of Indian Department more control over trade—often led to badly managed agreements or outright fraud. Consequently the Ioway headmen learned to distrust the government's ability to distribute goods to them. On many occasions the government failed to deliver much-needed supplies to the Ioways, leaving them destitute and desperately hungry. When the government failed to deliver food and supplies following the Ioways' move across the Missouri River in 1837, the tribe had been forced to turn to the traders Joseph Robidoux and James Gilmore, who stepped in to supply them with nearly two hundred dollars' worth of goods to help with the move. Such failures of the government were not uncommon.[29]

Often, when promised goods did arrive, they were either woefully inadequate in quantity or substandard in quality. In 1839 Indian Agent Jonathan Bean informed the Superintendent of Indian Affairs in St. Louis that the Ioways had "ridiculed, and not without abundant reason," the derringer pistols the department had sent them. They had requested hunting rifles. What they received instead was, according to Bean, "unlike anything I ever saw in the shape of an Indian Gun and absolutely a mockery of the article they were intended to represent and it appears to me they will never satisfy any Indians."[30]

Government oversight of the Great Nemaha Subagency reached a low point in 1838 and 1839. After Andrew Hughes was dismissed as subagent in January 1838 the post remained vacant for nearly two and a half years. Hughes's supervisor, John Dougherty (and his successor Joseph V. Hamilton), tried to manage the post from his station at the Bellevue Agency, nearly 125 miles away in present-day Nebraska, but the lack of direct supervision led to an even greater degree of confusion and mismanagement. Conditions became so chaotic that by late 1839 no one could determine with any degree of certainty who was rightfully employed at the subagency.[31]

No doubt frustrated with the chaos at the subagency, White Cloud and other Ioway headmen requested once again that they have full control over the money the government paid them each year. Furthermore they asked the government to dismiss everyone working at the subagency. Apparently the Ioways hoped this would give them some say in straightening out affairs at the subagency and in determining who the government rehired to fill the positions of farmer, interpreter, miller, and blacksmith. The request was denied, but a year later White Cloud, No Heart, Raining, and three other Ioway headmen signed an agreement that did give them some control over the scope of work the subagency farmer would perform each year.[32]

Three years later in a council with their new subagent, William Richardson, Ioway leaders discussed some of the challenges they were facing. Richardson called the council to discuss the Ioways' need to pay their debts, but the Ioways took the opportunity to touch on several topics with their subagent. Clearly the Ioways felt that their fortunes had declined since moving the subagency. They were still struggling with the government for control of their money, which by then amounted to twenty-five hundred dollars annually. By this time a major portion of their annuities went to pay the considerable debts they had incurred with traders. Raining admitted to Richardson, "We blame ourselves for going in debt, we all shared in what was bought and now we want all to share in paying. We will pay out what we can and divide the balance and be satisfied. We will try to pay up all our small debts and larger ones too if we can." The headman Kéramañi (Clearing Sky) explained that the Ioways had become so heavily indebted because "We used to depend on our hunting but we cannot now. We must rely on our money now."[33]

Richardson, however, worried that if the cash annuities were delivered directly to the headmen, they would squander a large portion of it on whiskey. The subagent's concerns were not without merit. The sale of contraband alcohol to the Ioways, Sacs, and Foxes was a problem that had plagued them long before they moved west of the Missouri River. Fur traders had long used whiskey as a ritual part of trade negotiations with Native people. Devious Europeans quickly learned that by plying Natives with alcohol they could impair their judgment and easily gain a substantial advantage in deal making. Over time heavy trade activity in the Missouri River valley led to overhunting and a dramatic decrease in animal populations. As the fur trade played out traders turned to liquor as a lucrative way to make money.

Even though the Trade and Intercourse Acts in 1804 outlawed the sale of alcohol to Natives, the practice continued unabated as unscrupulous traders found they could use alcohol to swindle Natives out of annuity money and whatever else they possessed. In 1835 a Sac man complained to Agent Dougherty, "[Our] young men hunted hard and killed but little, owing to the scarcity of game, and when they succeeded in collecting a few skins, and exchange them for a few goods, the whiskey smugglers come in with their kegs, make us drunk, and bear off everything we possess, and leave us to awaken from our drunken dreams naked and hungry."[34]

The Ioways, Sacs, and Foxes had hoped that by moving across the Missouri River they might free themselves from whiskey traders, but this proved not to be the case. Whiskey was simply too profitable and traders soon began shipping barrels across the river to Ioway Point. "Since we came here," reported the missionary William Hamilton in 1842, "the facilities for obtaining whiskey have been greatly increased, and the Indians are becoming yearly more intemperate." The storekeeper at Iowa Point told him that he had imported seventy-five barrels of whiskey that year. The Ioways' African American interpreter Jeffrey Deroine explained that profit margins were high enough to make the whiskey trade worth the risk of being caught, even though it was "not respectable."[35] By 1842 the Ioways' problem of losing annuity money to whiskey traders led Subagent Richardson to make the following ultimatum: "If, while paying out the annuities, I hear of one drop of whiskey being on this side [of the Missouri River] I will suspend payments for 6 months. I am tired of this whiskey. My patience is thin. You all know better. I beg of you to be sober at least a few months that you may see how much better you will be of and enjoy your living. You must not take *a single dram*. If I take *one* dram I want another and another and it is so with you. It is best to have *nothing* to do with it."[36]

On several occasions the Ioways tried to police themselves to keep from drinking. In March 1858, for example, Ioway headmen announced that anyone who got drunk before the spring planting was completed would be whipped. Elisha Dorian, the Ioways' mixed race interpreter, and another Ioway man broke the ban on alcohol and had to flee to Missouri to escape their punishment. Eventually the headmen agreed to let Dorian forgo the whipping if he agreed to provide a feast for tribal members.[37]

In addition to increasing their debt to whiskey traders, Richardson was concerned that the distribution of cash and annuities by tribal leaders would result in serious inequities. The subagent accused White Cloud and Jeffrey Deroine, who married White Cloud's niece, of using their power over the rest of the nation to take more than their share of the annuities:

It was evidently the wish of the Iowa[y]s that the money should have been paid to heads of families but they are so much afraid of Jeffrey and Frank [White Cloud] that they won't speak out. I hope to be ordered to make payment to the heads of the families. I am well satisfied it is their wish a very large majority, might say nine tenths. But if Jeffrey was interpreter and White Cloud would go with him around, nine tenths would say "give the money to Frank, he finds us when we are hungry and does our business."[38]

Deroine's close ties to White Cloud and other Ioways threatened Richardson's attempts to wrestle influence away from the young Ioway headman. The subagent leveled a number of charges against the interpreter, which he used as grounds for dismissing Deroine from employment with the Bureau of Indian Affairs. These charges included illegal trading with the Indians, selling whiskey, and using his position as interpreter to

turn the Ioways against the government. In November 1841 Richardson
fired Deroine and ordered him to leave the subagency. While Deroine
most likely retreated to his farm in Holt County, Missouri, just across the
river from the subagency, he maintained contact with White Cloud and
continued to play a role in the Ioways' affairs.[39]

In 1844 the influence of Francis White Cloud and his interpreter was
interrupted for more than two years when he and Deroine joined Raining,
Little Wolf, and eleven other Ioways on a trip to Europe with the painter
and showman George Catlin. In their absence No Heart acted as headman for the Ioways. Upon his return White Cloud encountered serious
challenges to his leadership powers. In April 1846 the new Superintendent of Indian Affairs in St. Louis, Thomas Harvey, traveled to the Great
Nemaha Subagency to deal with disciplinary issues related to subagency
employees. In a council with the Ioways on April 14, 1846, Harvey told
White Cloud that his friend Deroine must leave the subagency forever.
"Men ought not to keep bad company," Harvey explained. White Cloud
insisted that he had paid to free Deroine, who had been Joseph Robidoux's
slave until 1832, and he believed Deroine should be allowed to stay. "If
you have purchased him," responded Harvey, "you have done enough
for him."[40]

Harvey returned to the subagency in November 1846. He and yet another new subagent, William Rucker, were determined to end White
Cloud's influence and power over the Ioways. Harvey broke with traditional protocol by holding a council with all available members of the
Ioway Nation. In the council he asked that all those who wished to receive
their annuities from the subagent rather than from Francis White Cloud
to stand. After some initial hesitation Little Wolf stood in opposition to
his fellow headman. Following Little Wolf's lead all but a few Ioways stood.
From that point on, the government distributed annuities directly to all
heads of families within the tribe. Not only had White Cloud been publi-
cally humiliated, his role as a leader was permanently diminished.[41]

Instead of retreating, however, White Cloud launched an offensive
against the Great Nemaha Subagency, the Presbyterian mission, and
even against the Pawnees. In the spring of 1847 he enlisted John W. Kelly,
a white lawyer who lived across the river from the subagency in Oregon,
Missouri, to write to the Commissioner of Indian affairs on his behalf.
In the letter, which was signed by several Ioways, White Cloud lodged a

number of complaints about the subagency and the mission. He demanded
that Subagent Rucker remove the interpreter John Baptiste Roy and reinstate Deroine. Maintaining that Roy was a faulty translator White Cloud
said the Ioways desired an interpreter in whom they had confidence. In
the letter he asked why a mixed-race Ioway man named James Campbell
had been forced from the subagency and prophetically wondered when
the subagent might see fit to force him to leave.

The following year White Cloud attempted to regain his lost stature
among the Ioways by leading a violent attack against the Pawnees. In May
1848 he led a party of ninety-five warriors north to participate in an ambush that ended in the deaths of ten Pawnees, seven of whom were women
and children. After the fact No Heart and Raining claimed they had tried
to stop the ambush but White Cloud defended his actions by claiming
that a Pawnee raid on the Ioways' horses had precipitated the attack. He
further defended his actions by pointing out he had not expected the
government to condemn the Ioways for killing Pawnees since the U.S.
military had been responsible for many Pawnee deaths in the past. Hadn't
the Ioways, White Cloud reasoned, helped the military by attacking a
common enemy?[42]

While the attack led Superintendent of Indian Affairs Harvey to sever
all diplomatic recognition of White Cloud as an Ioway leader, many in the
tribe embraced him. For them the war party against a longtime enemy
had proved cathartic, providing the warriors a rare opportunity to participate in battle. Perhaps emboldened by his newfound success White
Cloud launched threats against the subagent and the missionaries, all of
whom he vowed to drive from the area. He removed his own children from
the mission school and threatened to remove all other Ioway children, by
force if necessary. Despite being arrested on charges of inciting violence
among the Ioways, he still wielded a great deal of power among his people
as late as 1849. In December 1851 Francis White Cloud died at the age of
forty. While the exact circumstances of his death remain unclear, it is generally believed that he was killed in an armed conflict with Pawnees.[43]

Since White Cloud had been shut out of his leadership role after the
attack on the Pawnees, No Heart already held the position of head chief
of the Ioways. In his mid-fifties at the time of White Cloud's death in 1851,
No Heart had been a consistent presence in the ranks of Ioway leadership
for two decades and would retain that position until his death in 1862.

Whereas White Cloud's exploits against the Pawnees had led some whites to describe him as a "fiend" and a "barbarous" butcher, they characterized No Heart as "an excellent man," who enjoyed "the confidence of his people, and the respect of the whites." Although sometimes overshadowed by his more turbulent nephew, No Heart seemed a stable force in his actions with the United States on behalf of his people. He was the only headman to make his mark on each of the five treaties the Ioways had with the United States between 1836 and 1861.[44]

After his nephew's death No Heart succeeded in mending relationships with the Pawnees and other Native nations. Under his leadership the Ioways made friendly visits to nearby agencies and reservations and continued to travel for their traditional buffalo hunts. In the fall of 1857 the Ioways visited their relatives the Otoes, who presented their visitors with sixty horses and other gifts. That same fall the Mississippi River branch of the Sacs, who lived along the Marais des Cygnes River in Kansas, paid the Ioways a visit for "a grand pow-wow and smoke." As late as 1858 the Ioways trekked hundreds of miles, apparently without incident, "in the direction of the rocky Mountains" to hunt buffalo.[45]

During the last decade of his life whites considered No Heart to be the last remaining hereditary headman or "chief" of the Ioways. He shared decision-making for the nation with a small group of headmen. The most prominent of these was Little Wolf who had become a leader through his prowess as a warrior. The missionary William Hamilton assessed that Little Wolf, deemed by some to be the most intelligent of the Ioway leaders, "has nearly all the mind of the company and though he is not treacherous, [he is] a little slippery." Also in the council was Ragráshe (British), whom Hamilton believed would do whatever Little Wolf believed was right, and Wamúnuge (the Man Who Steals). This group would lead the Ioway delegation in negotiating a new land cession with the United States in 1854.[46]

No Heart and his council faced severe challenges during the decade of the 1850s. Their people were decimated by disease, starvation, and violence, even more than when they moved to the subagency fifteen years earlier. Numbering between three and four hundred people, the Ioway nation was less than half the size it had been in 1837. Beginning in 1849, cholera, smallpox, and whooping cough all made their way to the Great Nemaha Agency via the Oregon Trail. Records of Ioway mortality are

British, also known as Ragrášhe, Laggarash, and Naggaresh, ca. 1880. British was a leader of the Ioways at a time when the United States asked them to relinquish the Great Nemaha Agency. Acting as second headman under No Heart during the negotiations for the Treaty of 1854, he helped persuade the government to allow the Ioways to remain on their agency rather than remove them to the Indian Territory. (Friends Historical Library of Swarthmore College.)

extremely rare. Settlers often made note of the number of white emigrants who died of disease near the agency but almost never tallied the deaths of Natives. In May 1851 the *St. Joseph Gazette* estimated from thirty to forty deaths of emigrants and settlers "near the city." That same month agent Richardson reported that smallpox had killed one-seventh of the Sacs and Foxes on the agency and was rapidly spreading among the Ioways. "I fear that it will sweep off a greater portion of that tribe." Assuming Richardson's fears were realized, disease could have killed as many as fifty to sixty Ioways that year. The agent hired a physician to vaccinate the Ioways, Sacs, and Foxes, but it is unlikely that they otherwise received regular medical care. In December 1854 Samuel Irvin wrote that the Ioways had lost 5 percent of their population since the end of the summer. If his estimate was correct that there were less than three hundred Ioways alive then fifteen had died in four short months.[47]

The Ioways' misery was further compounded by the fact that they were desperately poor and struggling to feed and clothe themselves. In 1854 Agent Daniel Vanderslice expressed his concern over the Ioways' dire condition to Commissioner of Indian Affairs George Manypenny. The agent noted that while the Ioways were making a good effort to live off the food they raised, "they must necessarily suffer much long before their summer crops mature." To help supplement their meager diets, Sacs, Foxes, and Ioways were often forced to feed on the cast-off leftover food of settlers and emigrants. In December 1848 artist Rudolph Kurz noted that the Ioways had set up a camp of about thirty lodges across the Missouri River from St. Joseph. He explained that because "wild animals were nigh exterminated" in the region the Ioways were not able to sustain themselves by hunting. "Winter is a difficult time for the Indians," he lamented, adding that the Ioways had located their camp near St. Joseph "for the benefit of the clippings and cuttings of meat and the wastage incident upon the hog killings season."[48]

The Ioways' resourcefulness in finding food was something that white settlers found both curious and stomach-turning. Many were surprised by the way Ioways begged for and collected settlers' food scraps. Sol Miller, the editor of the *White Cloud Kansas Chief*, made light of the way in which they picked up food remnants after the town's 1857 Fourth of July barbeque. "We doubt whether they even left enough picking for the pigs." Miller made the Ioways' desperate scavenging a running joke in the pages of the *Chief.* Whether hit by lightning or drowned while crossing the river, he reported, dead livestock was always likely to attract hungry Natives:

> Sometimes the Indians are "hard up" for eatables, when they hear of a carcass which has been lying in the sun for about a week. They straightway hunt it up, drive away the buzzards, and cutting it in pieces, carry it home in their wallets, and have a grand feast. . . . [They] gather up the scraps of bread, meat cake, pickles, etc, which are tumbled in together, and carried off for another feast! If dirt makes people healthy, no wonder these Indians are a robust race. But what is the use of buzzards, in this country?[49]

Violence, much of it initiated by alcohol, also exacted its toll on the Ioways. More than one Ioway died while attempting to cross the Missouri River to visit Old Pete, a free African American whiskey trader who lived on the Missouri shore. Miller's *Chief* reported that Old Pete "has been for some years engaged in selling whiskey to the Indians, and has had a drunken gang of them continually about him." Several shootings and stabbings involving Ioways occurred at the post. The *Chief* described an incident in which John Ma-hee, Hu-toy (who also went by the name Lowry), and other Ioway men confronted Old Pete after the trader had stabbed one of his Ioway customers. Tempers flared and Hu-toy shot Pete, leaving him with a flesh wound in the scalp. Pete retaliated by stabbing Hu-toy and killing him. In the last six months of 1860, Miller reported there had been seven or eight alcohol-related murders on Ioway land. "The Iowas have been dying and killed off very rapidly, within a few years past," the publisher opined, "and soon there will be none of them left. Whiskey is destroying them."[50]

No Heart's death by natural causes in 1862 marked another watershed for the Ioways. After that point the United States would no longer recognize a hereditary chief among the Ioways. Even though Francis White Cloud's son Robert was poised to inherit the position as head chief, there were several White Cloud descendants who desired to challenge him for the position. Subsequently a power struggle developed within the tribe. John A. Burbank, the tribe's agent between 1861 and 1866, hand-picked the headman British to represent the Ioway in treaty negotiations and other official business with the United States. It seems British won Burbank's favor in large part because of his seniority (he had been second chief under No Heart and had long served on the tribal council), though one wonders—based on Hamilton's earlier assessment—if the subagent hoped British would continue leading as No Heart had done. Whites described the new Ioway leader as eloquent, and it seems he won the hearts of many of those who lived near the agency. Speaking once to a crowd of whites in the new village of White Cloud, British said he had given all this land to the white men and only kept a little up by the Nemaha River for himself. He claimed to have killed more than one hundred men and stolen many horses, but he assured the citizens of White Cloud that he was a friend to the white men and a friend to their new settlement.[51]

The United States had long believed that Indian tribes would benefit from breaking the line of hereditary leaders. As early as 1825 William Clark wrote that he believed it was important for the U.S. government to encourage the Indian nations to adopt a structure of leadership based on elected civil authority. He thought a civil government would help to unify tribes like the Ioways, and he hoped that an elected government would also make life within tribes more peaceful. "It is believed," Clark wrote to Secretary of War James Barbour, "that executive agents of this authority will prevent Indians from killing one another for the Chief place, and keep the inferior officers . . . within the bounds of their duty." Clark reminded the secretary that if these reforms proved successful, the U.S. government would no longer need to support Indian nations with annuities. This, he wrote, would allow the United States to "free the treasury from what would otherwise remain an everlasting charge upon it."[52]

Civil government would not be fully adopted by the Ioways until the Indian Reorganization Act took effect in the 1930s. In the seven decades between No Heart's death and the adoption of the Ioways' constitutions, the Bureau of Indian Affairs and the local agents exercised unprecedented power over the tribe's business dealings and took every opportunity to undercut the Ioway's ability to govern themselves. However, the government's paternalistic attempts to exercise control over the tribe was seriously compromised by fraud, greed, politics, and incompetence.

CHAPTER 5

Crooked Fathers and Neglected Children

The Ioways' new home on the Great Nemaha Subagency allowed the federal government to intervene more efficiently in all facets of their religious, civic, and economic lives. While the agents of the Office of Indian Affairs were confident that they could teach the Ioways to live in the manner of their "civilized" non-Native neighbors, the correspondence in the office's files indicates otherwise.[1] Subagents, their employees, and their supervisors seem to have been far more concerned with protecting their own careers, lining their pockets, helping their allies, and staining the reputations of their enemies than they were in tending to the business of improving the Ioways' lives. At the Great Nemaha Subagency political patronage, ineptitude, and outright fraud seriously compromised the government's ability to carry out its mission of Indian reform successfully.

This was in no small part because of the Indian office's unwieldy organizational structure and the fact that it was largely a political machine. When the Ioways, Sacs, and Foxes arrived at their new home, their assigned subagent was Andrew S. Hughes, who had a long history with these three nations as he had served as agent at the old Ioway Agency in Missouri since 1828. Hughes's supervisor was the Indian agent of the Missouri River, John Dougherty, another longtime Indian office employee, who was posted 125 miles north of the Great Nemaha Subagency at the Upper Missouri Indian Agency near present-day Bellevue, Nebraska. Dougherty, in turn,

reported to the Superintendent of Indian Affairs in St. Louis. At the time
the Ioways were moving to their new agency in 1837, William Clark had
held that position for nearly three decades. Clark died in 1838, however,
and was replaced by fur trader Joshua Pilcher. Clark and Pilcher answered
directly to the Commissioner of Indian affairs in Washington who in
1837 was Carey A. Harris. Because the Office of Indian Affairs was then a
branch of the Department of War, Harris answered to the secretary of
war, a cabinet member who in turn reported directly to the president.
In the spring of 1837 a newly inaugurated president of the United States,
Martin Van Buren, was in the process of appointing a new secretary of
war, Joel Roberts Poinsett.

Fifteen hundred miles of rugged terrain separated one end of this bureaucratic chain of command from the other, and messages sent from
Washington could take three weeks to reach the Great Nemaha Subagency.
While this all but ensured that decisions were made and orders executed
at a glacial pace, it proved an efficient funnel for political patronage.
Changing political winds in Washington, D.C., could be felt as far away as
the shores of the Missouri River. Because Kansas was not yet a state in
1837, most of those political winds blew through Missouri, and subagents
often found their political fortunes tied not only to Washington but to
Show-me-state politics as well.

Government oversight of the Great Nemaha Subagency seems to have
been flawed from the outset. When nearly one thousand Ioways and five
hundred Sacs and Foxes moved there in the spring of 1837 with hopes of
settling down in time to plant crops for the coming year, it was immediately apparent that, while the government had been eager to push the Natives out of Missouri, it had done nothing to prepare for their arrival in
present-day Kansas. Since there were no boundary lines to indicate which
portion of the new subagency belonged to the Ioways and which belonged
to the Sacs and Foxes, the tribes located their villages along the Missouri
River, near the mouth of the Wolf River in what is now Doniphan County,
Kansas. Isaac McCoy finally arrived to survey the subagency in July and,
finding the new residents already settled, marked out a dog-legged boundary
line to separate the Ioways from the Sacs and Foxes. Because land west of
the Missouri River had not yet been surveyed by the General Land Office,
McCoy was not bound to run his lines in accordance with the federal grid
system. This would create trouble when federal surveyors marked out the

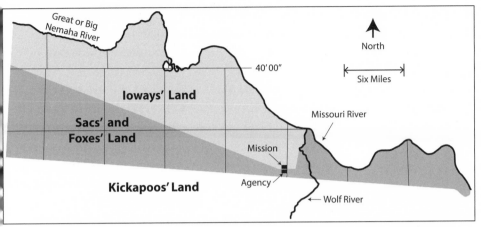

The boundaries of the Great Nemaha Subagency (later Agency), 1837–54. The subagency had not been surveyed when the Sacs, Foxes, and Ioways arrived in the spring of 1837. With no guidance on where to settle, the new residents selected their own village sites near the Wolf River. When Isaac McCoy arrived to make his survey a few months later, he had to loop the boundary lines between the Ioways and the Sacs and Foxes. This accounts for the unusual shape of the boundary lines. (Map by the author. Copyright © 2016, University of Oklahoma Press.)

territory twenty years later. Perhaps for this reason McCoy's handiwork earned the ire of at least one fellow surveyor, who remarked years later, "McCoy never did anything right and his blunder has already caused [the subagency] very great trouble."[2]

McCoy had barely set his survey stakes in the ground by the time the first of many controversies involving Great Nemaha subagents erupted. By late 1837 rumors circulating within Missouri's political circles alleged that Subagent Hughes was a habitual drunk. There seems to be little evidence to substantiate this accusation, but the charge of intemperance was commonly leveled against those employed at the subagency. Such a claim not only had the potential to soil a man's moral reputation, it could also imply that the subagent was sympathetic to, if not in collusion with, the whiskey traders that preyed on the Ioways. This was important because subagents also doubled as law enforcement officials on Indian land. Often they were the only legal deterrent standing between the Natives and the whiskey traders. To make matters worse, all subagents found themselves caught between powerful Missouri commercial interests, which made a great deal of money selling whiskey to Native people, and those political parties that were vehemently opposed to the sale of alcohol in Indian territory. A subagent need only choose one of the two sides to unleash the wrath of the other.[3]

A second charge accused Hughes of having advised the Ioways not to sign the Treaty of 1837 in which they ceded the western third of the present-day state of Iowa to the United States. Indeed the treaty negotiations in Washington had become a diplomatic debacle. The Ioways believed that the Sacs and Foxes of the Mississippi, led by Keokuk, were trying to sell land to the government without acknowledging that the Ioways had a legitimate claim to it as well. They were further incensed by their perception that the treaty commissioners were deceiving them. In the weeks leading up to the negotiations William Clark stated that Hughes had more influence with the Ioways than any man living. Commissioners in Washington hoped that the subagent might be able to bring the Ioways to the table to sign the treaty. When the Ioways angrily left Washington, D.C., before talks could be concluded, however, Hughes took the blame. Only after the delegation reached St. Louis on its way home was Clark able to persuade them to finally sign the document.[4]

More serious, perhaps, were suspicions that Subagent Hughes had been padding the subagency census by as much as 100 percent and was conspiring with the traders to use the inflated numbers to procure extra supplies from the government, which he could then sell on the black market. Hughes, who had served as subagent for the Ioways under the Democratic administrations of presidents John Quincy Adams, Andrew Jackson, and Martin Van Buren, vehemently denied all three charges against him and blamed the rumors on Whig activists in Missouri who were working to undermine popular support for the state's Democratic governor Lilburn Boggs, and its venerable U.S. senator Thomas Hart Benton.

Despite the fact that Hughes had the support of members of the Missouri Democratic congressional delegation, his relationship with his supervisor John Dougherty, a staunch Whig, had never been particularly good. As the controversy worsened Hughes wrote to Commissioner of Indian Affairs Harris to offer his resignation. If Hughes had hopes of being reinstated as Indian agent, those hopes ended when his supporter William Clark died in September 1838. Both Dougherty and Pilcher—longtime rivals—actively sought to succeed Clark as Superintendent of Indian Affairs in St. Louis. Through his political connections Pilcher won the backing of Senator Benton and secured the position. Pilcher, who did not like Hughes, made no attempt to clear the agent of the charges against him.[5]

Pilcher took his time finding a replacement for Hughes. From January 1838 until June 1840, a period of twenty-nine months, the subagency hung in bureaucratic limbo with no subagent. The Office of Indian Affairs chose to allow the agent of the Upper Missouri Indian Agency to oversee the Great Nemaha Subagency's operation. However, soon after failing to receive the promotion he sought, John Dougherty resigned as Indian Agent of the Upper Missouri, and Pilcher assigned Joseph V. Hamilton to fill the vacancy. Upon arrival at his new post, Hamilton found that Dougherty had left the Upper Missouri Indian Agency in disarray. It did not appear that agency employees had been actively working for some time and nearly all government property had apparently disappeared.[6]

Given Hamilton's preoccupation with restoring order at his own post, it is reasonable to assume he had little time to manage the Great Nemaha Subagency. Still, Pilcher's failure to hire someone to directly oversee the welfare of the Ioways, Sacs, and Foxes is surprising. Perhaps Pilcher refused to act because he viewed the Ioways with some disdain, referring to them as a "very troubled band of Indians." He complained to Commissioner of Indian Affairs T. Hartley Crawford, "These people have had farmers, missionaries, and teachers for twelve or fifteen years . . . and I defy the world to point to a single beneficial result."[7] Despite Pilcher's misgivings, the Indian office was bound by treaty to retain a staff of blacksmiths, farmers, teachers, and interpreters to ensure that the Great Nemaha subagency continued to operate. Nonetheless, the combination of Pilcher's spite and Hamilton's neglect caused conditions there to quickly deteriorate.

By the late summer of 1838 the Indian office had lost track of just who was in charge of dispensing annuities and provisions to the subagency's Native population. In August Pilcher sent Jonathan Bean, who had preceded Hughes as the Ioway's agent, to the Great Nemaha Subagency to make sure that government suppliers were making good on their contracts and that the supplies they had delivered were safe. When Bean arrived, he found the operation in near total disorder and the Ioways "extremely bad[ly] disposed" toward the "government and their good intentions toward them." In his report to Pilcher in October 1838, Bean wrote that the Indians were "as different a people as you could possibly imagine from what they were, when I was their subagent in 1827 and 1828. In place of the mild friendly well-disposed people then, I find a distrustful, ill-natured, fierce and insolent people." He met with the headmen of the Sacs and Foxes and the Ioways in an attempt to regain their trust. "They complain about everything," Bean wrote to Pilcher. In particular, the Indians were unhappy with the manner in which their annuities and the government's procurement of trade goods for them had been mishandled in the absence of a regular subagent.[8]

Aside from dealing with the complaints of the Ioways, Sacs, and Foxes, Bean's first job was to determine who was legitimately employed at the subagency. Apparently, in the months after Hughes's dismissal, several individuals had appeared who claimed to be employees of the office. Bean quickly set about expelling everyone who could not prove they were government employees. The Ioways told Bean they were unhappy with the legitimate employees and asked him to dismiss them all. Bean discovered that, with the exception of the Presbyterian missionaries, most of the staff members were more than a little fed up with the chaotic atmosphere of the subagency and were happy to leave. Those who could write gladly drafted their resignations. Those who could not write allowed Bean to inform Pilcher of their intentions to leave. In an attempt make a clean start at conducting the business of the subagency, Bean then hired a new staff of farmers, blacksmiths, millers, and interpreters who he believed were disposed to remain loyal to the Indian department and the administration in Washington.[9]

The power vacuum that had been created by the absence of a subagent on the Great Nemaha Subagency had created one unanticipated consequence. It had endowed Samuel Irvin and William Hamilton, the Presbyterian missionaries, with a significant amount of newfound influence both with the Indians and with local government officials. Before his resignation Dougherty had hired Irvin to be an "issuing agent," who would make sure that government supplies reached the hands of the Ioways, Sacs, and Foxes. The missionaries also served as interpreters for the Ioway headmen and on occasion even conducted councils with them. In a September 1840 council, for example, Irvin acted as the government's representative in an agreement in which he promised to provide the Ioways with a farmer. As a result the missionaries gained a level of influence that would prove a source of irritation to future Ioway subagents for the next two decades.[10]

Finally, in June 1840, the Indian office hired Congrave Jackson from the Osage Subagency on the upper Neosho River to manage the Great Nemaha Subagency. Jackson was unable to complete his business with the Osages for several months and did not arrive at his new post until November 15, 1840. Less than nine months later Jackson was gone. The reason for his brief tenure is unclear, though it was likely related to the political changes in Washington. In March 1841 Whig General William Henry Harrison entered the White House. Due to Harrison's death one month later, his Vice-President John Tyler succeeded him as president in April. T. Hartley Crawford, an appointee of Democrat Martin Van Buren, retained his position as the Commissioner of Indian affairs in Washington, but David D. Mitchell quickly replaced Pilcher as the Superintendent of Indian Affairs in St. Louis and, on August 4, 1841, a staunch Whig by the name of William Richardson took the position of Great Nemaha Subagent.[11]

Richardson appears to have been one of the most severely paternalistic of the early subagents and his determination to reform the Ioways' behavior led him to extremes that included occasional beatings and floggings. John McNamara, an Episcopal missionary in western Missouri, once described Richardson as a "large, fierce-looking man, [who was] long accustomed to kick[ing] and cuff[ing] poor Negroes and Indians."[12]

Within months of his arrival at the subagency, Richardson was embroiled in a confrontation with Ioway headman Francis White Cloud. The standoff was the result of the ongoing disagreement between the Ioways and the government over the manner in which their annuities were to be distributed. Richardson viewed the annuities as a tool that could be used to leverage positive behavior from the Ioways. He had threatened to withhold them for six months if tribal members did not stop drinking and associating with whiskey traders. In his 1842 annual report to Mitchell, Richardson vented his frustration: "It is useless for me to scold them . . . they confess it is wrong, but transgress perhaps the next day or at least as soon as an opportunity should offer. It is utterly useless for me to try to keep them from whiskey."[13]

Richardson's relations with White Cloud were further damaged when the subagent fired the Ioways' interpreter and White Cloud's friend Jeffrey

Deroine in November 1841 on the grounds that Deroine was taking advantage of his connections with the Ioways and selling them whiskey. "I am full[y] persuaded that as long as Jeffrey has any communication or influence with the Ioways, they will not improve in any way."[14] Deroine left the service of the Indian office, but he remained in the area and, much to Richardson's chagrin, continued to have some influence over White Cloud and the Ioways. The situation was eased somewhat by the fact that the two men left for their two-year trip to Europe in 1844 and did not return until after Richardson's dismissal.

Although he feuded with the Native people under his charge, Richardson claimed affection for them and lauded the efforts of the "benevolent and pious" missionaries Hamilton and Irvin for forgoing their own comfort "for the sole purpose of bettering the condition of these unfortunate children of the forest." He bitterly complained about the Ioways' behavior, about being physically threatened by whiskey traders, and about having to repair the residence on the subagency at his own expense, but Richardson seemed eager to retain his position as subagent. After Democrat James K. Polk won the 1844 presidential election, calls for Richardson's dismissal soon surfaced as did rumors about the physical abuse he occasionally meted out. Richardson's sensitivity to the rumors verged on the paranoiac. In January 1845 he contacted Missouri congressman James M. Hughes, a Democrat, and threatened to make public certain information he claimed to have regarding fraud perpetrated by former Subagent Hughes— apparently no relation to the congressman—should the Democrats chose to remove him from his position.[15]

After months of receiving no definitive confirmation as to whether he would be replaced or retained, Richardson sent a letter of resignation directly to President Polk in July 1845. "I am well satisfied that you will be importuned by those who desire my situation until you cannot avoid removing me," he wrote, "and I much prefer fixing my own time to leave. . . . I have lived here for more than three years in this doubtful state of suspense and feel unwilling to endure it any longer." Richardson informed Polk that he personally knew at least three people who coveted his job. He believed one of these men was a St. Louis trader named McKee who hoped to turn the appointment into a cash cow for his company and concluded that he believed the president was in some way personally involved in a plot to oust him from the subagency. Richardson left his post at the end of September 1845. Taking most of the subagency's official records with him, he moved to nearby St. Joseph, Missouri, where he lived until he was reinstated as subagent four years later.[16]

Richardson's rocky tenure at the Great Nemaha Subagency seemed relatively placid compared to that of his immediate successor, Colonel Armstrong McClintock. While McClintock enjoyed the support of the Missouri Democrats, he immediately clashed with subagency employees and with the Presbyterian missionaries, who accused him, among other things, of being an incompetent atheist. The problem seems to have stemmed from an incident in which McClintock fired Andrew Meyer, the assistant blacksmith, for allegedly appropriating between thirty and forty pounds of government steel for his personal use. As Meyer had been hired by Richardson, the incident incensed the former subagent's Whig supporters. Richardson's backers were further outraged when they learned that McClintock dismissed the agency farmer, a man named John Foreman, and hired his own brother, Hugh McClintock, to take his place. The Whigs retaliated with a smear campaign against McClintock and with repeated calls for his dismissal. "All of Richardson's faction was let loose at me with all the bitterness of their Whig feelings," the subagent reported in December 1845.[17]

McClintock unwisely attempted to silence his opposition by requesting that a company of dragoons be deployed to the subagency to assist in removing all unwanted persons. The dismissal of government employees by such draconian means enraged both those employees who remained at the subagency and those who had been expelled. Both Irvin and John Foreman, the dismissed farmer, voiced their concerns about McClintock in letters sent directly to Superintendent of Indian Affairs in St. Louis Thomas H. Harvey. Alarmed by the accusations against his subordinate, Harvey visited the subagency in April 1846 to find out for himself the extent of the problem. He met in council with the Ioways and the Sacs and Foxes, interviewed other parties involved in the disagreement, and passed his findings on to Commissioner of Indian Affairs William Medill in Washington.[18]

Harvey met with the Ioways on April 10 and 14 in the newly completed mission school building. Only recently returned from Europe, White Cloud had not had time to become acquainted with McClintock or with the details of the subagent's scandal. He was concerned, however, with the fact that Foreman's dismissal would mean a delay in spring planting. "The difficulties with the missionaries and agent are strange to me," he told Harvey. "The missionaries [have] never done us any harm, but the agent refused to employ our farmer for us." The Ioways expressed their wish to hire a Mr. McKee to replace Foreman, but White Cloud and No Heart deferred to Harvey on the issue, preferring instead to steer the conversation toward the ongoing issue of debt and the government's control over their annuities. Harvey refused to give the Ioways an advance on their annuities but assured them that he would hire McKee to see to their fields immediately.[19]

In his final report to Commissioner Medill, Harvey determined that McClintock's behavior had been inappropriate on several counts. He reported that the subagent's firing of John Foreman had been a clear case of nepotism. Harvey further judged that the subagent had not had just cause in requesting assistance from the dragoons in expelling other former employees. Finally the superintendent reported that he had quite by accident uncovered at least two cases of financial mismanagement on the part of McClintock. First, Harvey reported that McClintock had made a "poorly considered" cash advance of their annuities to the Sacs and Foxes and, second, that he had fraudulently contracted a vendor to provide coal for the subagency, which he knew would never be delivered. When Harvey confronted McClintock with these accusations, the agent admitted that he had made mistakes and offered his resignation effective June 1, 1846.[20]

McClintock had not been without his supporters. Bella Hughes, the daughter of former Subagent Hughes, wrote to Secretary of War William Marcy to express her outrage at the accusations against McClintock. She claimed Samuel Irvin and William Hamilton, the Presbyterian missionaries, were the source of the charges against the subagent. "As long as the [Presbyterians] are permitted to locate among the Indians," she wrote, "may your department be expected to be in constant receipt of malicious charges against its officers." Obviously stung by the events that had ended her father's career eighteen years earlier, she claimed that McClintock was the victim of "those who . . . profess the mild religion of our savior . . . [yet] . . . are continually whiling their fangs to do evil."[21]

Missouri lawyer George R. Gibson reported that he too believed the missionaries had been behind the charges against McClintock. According to Gibson, Irvin and Hamilton lived a comfortable life on the subagency and had turned the mission farm into a money-making operation at the expense of the Ioways. To maintain their status, Gibson alleged, the missionaries had "acted badly toward . . . McClintock" and "prejudiced and poisoned the mind of Major Harvey." He contended that the missionaries induced Harvey to visit the agency and misled him about the events that took place there, adding that they sought to exercise influence over the superintendent and to have the subagent "under their thumb." "The Missionaries," wrote Gibson, "are either actuated by improper motive, or they are incompetent to manage an institution which is avowedly and presumably for the benefit alone of the Indians."[22]

At least one prominent Missouri Democrat subscribed to this view as well. Former U.S. congressman James M. Hughes told Commissioner Medill that "the missionaries were determined from the time Col. McClintock was first appointed [as subagent] to sacrifice him," because they had been "exceedingly vexed" by Richardson's dismissal. The missionaries admitted to no political party affiliations, but Irvin and Hamilton had been strong supporters of McClintock's predecessor, William Richardson. The missionaries considered Richardson to be a "warm and untiring friend" and observed that he was the only subagent during their tenure that had taken an interest in the Indians and in the mission. They had apparently protested to the Polk administration when Richardson left the subagency and, in the eyes of some observers, were set against McClintock from the beginning.[23]

William Rucker replaced McClintock in June 1846 and served as subagent at the Great Nemaha Subagency for twenty-one months. Like his predecessor Rucker soon became the target of a Whig campaign of rumors against him. Less than six months after Rucker's appointment, Commissioner Medill in Washington received a letter purported to have been written by Samuel C. Hall, one of St. Joseph's leading Democrats, charging Rucker with intemperance. Perhaps determined not to let the Whigs undermine the career of another of their government employees, Missouri Democrats quickly countered the charges against Rucker. U.S. senator David Rice Atchison forwarded a letter from Hall to Commissioner Medill in which Hall denied writing the letter that made accusations against Rucker. Obviously angry Hall vowed that he would "ferret out the infamous puppy who would dare use my name without my consent or knowledge."[24]

Unlike McClintock, Rucker enjoyed the backing of the Presbyterian missionaries and several subagency employees. Reverend Irvin wrote Medill to express his belief that the challenges against Rucker's character were the product of the subagent's staunch opposition to the sale of whiskey to Indians. In a letter that was cosigned by seven employees of the Great Nemaha Subagency, Irvin reported that "the enmity . . . of the whiskey traders against Major Rucker sufficiently shows his opposition" to the consumption of alcohol and proved his innocence.[25]

In April 1847, however, Secretary of War Marcy received a letter from a Missouri attorney named John Kelly in which Kelly claimed the Ioways were very dissatisfied with their subagent, the missionaries, the government, and especially with Superintendent of Indian Affairs in St. Louis Thomas Harvey. Kelly claimed that several Ioway headmen sought him out and asked him to draft the letter directly to the secretary because they had "little faith or confidence" in Harvey's ability to faithfully deliver their message of dissatisfaction to Washington. In the letter, Kelly wrote:

I have no doubt but those Indians have been shamefully swindled and wronged for sometime past, but by whom it is not my province to say at present. The whiskey traders charge it to the Missionaries and traders among the Indians, and the missionaries and traders among the Indians in return charge it on the whiskey traders on the border. I have no doubt of the charge against the whiskey traders being truth, and I have strong reasons to believe that the charge against the Missionaries and traders among the Ioway has some foundation.[26]

William Rucker managed to weather the storm of controversy that surrounded him at the agency for eleven more months. He left on March 1, 1848, though it is unclear whether he departed willingly or was forced to resign. The problems with whiskey traders also mired the tenure of Rucker's replacement Alfred J. Vaughan, who served as subagent until the fall of 1849. According to anthropologist Earnest Schusky, it seems Vaughan was not interested in engaging with the Native people under his charge while serving as subagent. Schusky has written that Vaughan "appears to have seen his job as primarily one of making the annuities distributions." Even after he left the Great Nemaha Subagency and became the agent at the Upper Missouri Indian Agency in 1853, Vaughan spent most of his time in St. Joseph, Missouri, only occasionally tending to business on the agency. Given this hands-off approach to his work, it is not surprising that reports reached Washington that Vaughan had become lax in stopping whiskey from reaching the Great Nemaha Subagency and that he had lost the confidence of some local politicians.[27]

The ongoing instability at the subagency was exacerbated by changes taking place in Washington in 1849. That year, the Office of Indian Affairs was transferred from the War Department to the newly created Department of the Interior. The legislation creating the department took effect just as Whig Zachary Taylor entered the White House in March 1849. Taylor nominated Thomas Ewing to be the first secretary of the interior and Orlando Brown to become the new Commissioner of Indian affairs. In St. Louis David Mitchell, who had previously served as Superintendent of Indian Affairs under Whig presidents William Henry Harrison and John Tyler, was reappointed to that position, replacing Thomas Harvey. Sensing the dissatisfaction with Great Nemaha Subagent Vaughan and expecting that the changes in Washington would filter down to the local level, a campaign began to reinstate William Richardson (who was living in St. Joseph) as subagent. Richardson himself wrote to Commissioner of Indian Affairs Brown defending his past conduct and reminding Brown that he had never embarrassed his party while serving as subagent. He also took pains to point out that, even though his daughter Ann had recently married Missouri Democratic congressman Willard P. Hall, he and Hall were not, and would never be, political allies.[28]

The missionaries Irvin and Hamilton wrote to Secretary of the Interior Ewing in support Richardson. "His open, efficient and honorable conduct not only justifies this recommendation," the missionaries wrote, "but has secured for him the love and confidence of the true friends of the Indians. The honor and interest of the department will, we doubt not, be well sustained in his hands." They further noted the rude manner in which Richardson had been previously dismissed, adding that such treatment entitled him receive a "high degree of attention" from the new Whig administration.[29]

Richardson was reinstated as the subagent for the Great Nemaha Subagency on December 18, 1849, just in time to oversee the implementation of a major bureaucratic reorganization of the Bureau of Indian Affairs.

On February 27, 1851, an act of Congress established a new Central Superintendency to take the place of the St. Louis Superintendency. This
new office remained in St. Louis, and David D. Mitchell retained his position as superintendent. The Great Nemaha Subagency became a full
agency and was expanded to include the Kickapoos, whose land adjoined
the Sacs and Foxes' southern border. The reorganization required that
Richardson be formally appointed to the position of agent. Hamilton and
Irvin wrote to their Presbyterian supervisors in Pennsylvania to ask that
they exercise whatever influence they may have in Washington to as-
sure that Richardson got the job, even though there seems to have been
little opposition to retaining him. Richardson became a full agent when the
reorganization took effect on July 1, 1851.[30]

After the inauguration of Democratic president Franklin Pierce in
March 1853, Richardson left his position as agent but remained a powerful force in the region. As momentum grew for the creation of the Kansas
Territory, Richardson became active in so-called squatters groups, which
petitioned the government to open land west of the Missouri River for settlement. He later became a general in the Kansas territorial militia and a
council member in the territory's proslavery "bogus legislature."[31]

The creation of the Kansas Territory and pressure to open the territory to white settlers occupied much of the tenure of Daniel Vanderslice,
who became Richardson's successor at the Great Nemaha Agency on
April 18, 1853. Movement to survey the land for settlement had led to a
discussion of a treaty that would remove the Ioways, Sacs, and Foxes from
their agency. The missionaries worried that the Indians' displacement
would jeopardize the future of their mission and lobbied hard to ensure
the agency remained intact.[32] Aside from worries about their own welfare,
however, Irvin and Hamilton expressed legitimate concerns that corrupt
traders were driving a proposed treaty between the residents of the agency
and the federal government. Irvin claimed that traders were working in
collaboration with Vanderslice and that the new Commissioner of Indian
Affairs, George Manypenny, though well-meaning, was surrounded by
crooked clerks in Washington and would be unable to effectively intervene
on behalf of the Native residents.[33]

In 1853 three traders were licensed to conduct business on the Great
Nemaha Agency. They were Joseph Robidoux, who had traded with the
Ioways for decades, William Hughes, and former agency farmer John

CROOKED FATHERS AND NEGLECTED CHILDREN

Foremen. Irvin did not specify which of these traders was involved in the corruption, but he alleged that the traders who sold goods to the Ioways had rigged the system so that each year, "the Ioways were indebted to the traders more than the full amount of their annuities." Several Ioways had informed Irvin that Vanderslice and the traders were pressuring them to pay off their debts. If they failed to do so, the trader told them "they would not get one dollar of credit this fall and they would perish in the winter." The unnamed trader also explained that he had "great influence in Washington and would use it in the coming treaty if [the Ioways] didn't pay him." Irvin believed that the push to collect the Ioways' debts was part of a plan in which Vanderslice's son was preparing to go into partnership with one of the licensed traders. By collecting all outstanding debts, the new partnership, which Irvin calculated could make three thousand dollars a year, could start business with a clean set of books.[34]

In May 1854 while Congress was debating the Kansas-Nebraska Act, which established the Kansas Territory, a delegation of Ioway, Sac, and Fox headmen accompanied by Agent Vanderslice were also in Washington, meeting with officials from the Bureau of Indian Affairs. The talks concluded with a treaty that left the agency intact but reduced it to one-quarter its original size. The Sacs and Foxes relinquished all of their land on the agency. The Ioways gave up one-half of theirs and agreed to share the remaining half with the displaced Sacs and Foxes. The land these tribes had given up was to be surveyed and sold at public auction. The proceeds from these sales would be held in trust by the government. The Ioways, Sacs, and Foxes would receive payments from this trust fund at the president's discretion.[35]

While the Ioways lost much in the Treaty of 1854, others profited handsomely. Their interpreter, John Baptiste Roy, received a grant of 320 acres. Roy was allowed to select the land himself. He chose land in a wooded area known as Wolf Grove, which was located about two miles northwest of the mission. The Presbyterian Board of Foreign Missionaries was given 320 acres of land surrounding the mission and an additional 160 acres of timber land. Like Roy, the Presbyterians were granted the right to choose the land they wanted.[36]

Others also received or attempted to receive choice parcels of land at greatly reduced prices, though their names do not appear on any treaty. John Foreman, the trader and former agency farmer, quickly bought Roy's land grant and wasted no time in proposing a land deal with the Board of Foreign Missionaries. Foreman asked the missionaries to locate their 160-acre timber grant at the site of Iowa Point, a small village and river port located about five miles north of the mission on the Missouri River. Because it was the center of transportation and commerce on the agency, Iowa Point was easily one of the most desirable parcels of land in the area. The settlement was also the location of Foreman's trading house. Betting that once the region was open to white settlement, Iowa Point would become a thriving town, Foreman proposed to trade the Presbyterians 240 acres of his Wolf Point land in exchange for 160 acres at Iowa Point.[37]

It appears that the Presbyterians accepted some form of Foreman's proposal, because six months later Irvin wrote the Board of Foreign Missionaries asking to purchase 100 of the 320 acres of land the board then owned at Wolf Grove. Irvin lamented that he had not taken full advantage of the land bonanza created by the 1836 Platte Purchase. Aside for some undeveloped lots he owned in St. Joseph, "I have no land in the world I can call my own," he complained. "I have a little helpless family of five," he wrote to the Walter Lowrie, the board's corresponding secretary, "and were I called away from them now, they have no place on earth they can call a home." On March 11, 1857, Irvin signed a title to sixty acres of the Wolf Grove land. He paid five dollars per acre for forty acres and ten dollars per acre for the remaining twenty.[38]

One of the men who profited the most from the Treaty of 1854 was Agent Vanderslice. The public sale of the land ceded in the treaty finally took place in 1857. Slightly more than 94,000 acres were sold at auction for less than two dollars an acre. After the initial offering, some 1,122 acres remained unsold. Among the unsold land was the Sacs' 200-acre farm located just south of the mission site. The fact that the land remained unsold was surprising given that it had been cultivated and improved with buildings and fencing at the expense of the federal government. In fact, Daniel Vanderslice had withheld the farm from public sale until his tenure on the agency had nearly ended in 1862. He then quietly placed the farm on the market without advertising the sale to the public. On the day of the sale, a close acquaintance of Vanderslice's bought the farm for seven dollars and fifty cents an acre and sold the land to the subagent the next day for ten dollars an acre.[39] Vanderslice claimed to have been careful to distance himself from speculators and claimed that those who criticized him for his land dealings did so because he had "refused them privileges" in buying land. "Yet with all my care to avoid even the appearance of sinister motives in the performance of any part of my duty," he asserted, "I have been gravely charged with keeping off settlers from the Iowa Trust Lands and for the purpose of holding it for my friends and relatives."[40]

The ethnographer Lewis Henry Morgan, who visited the Great Nemaha Agency at the time of the sale, expressed outrage over Vanderslice's outright act of fraud and the government's failure to punish him for it. "Even now he passes for an honest man," an incensed Morgan wrote after the sale. He chastised the government for allowing the Ioways' land be sold at a fraction of its market price and worried that such wanton lack of oversight severely compromised the government's program of Indian reform. "So much for experimental farms," Morgan wrote, "and the history of this farm is the history of all [agency farms]."[41]

Morgan's observations appear to sum up much of the problem with the operation of the Great Nemaha Agency. It seems that greed or incompetence undercut any hope of making a positive change in the lives of the Ioways, Sacs, or Foxes. Controversy and scandal were the rule rather than the exception, as politics seemed to gain an increasingly strong hold over the workings of the agency and the Bureau of Indians Affairs. Left behind in the scuffle for power and favor were the Ioways, who sank further into poverty.

CHAPTER 6

Expanding Horizons and Constricting Boundaries

For the Ioways the nineteenth century was a time of dramatic loss of land and deepening poverty. We saw how a series of treaties and land cessions removed the Ioway people, who once claimed most of present-day Iowa and northern Missouri as their own, to the two-hundred-square-mile Great Nemaha Subagency. Yet even after they arrived at the subagency, the Ioways' landholdings continued to diminish. Poverty, coercion, and outright fraud during the 1840s and 1850s forced the Ioways to relinquish much of what little land they had, in order to make it available to non-Native settlers. What is more, pressure from the U.S. government during these decades forced the Ioways to begin a transformation that would steer them away from village life and communal farming toward lives as yeoman farmers occupying independent plots of land.

Yet just as the constricting limitations of land cessions and U.S. government policies seemed to make the Ioways' world infinitely smaller and more restricted, a curious thing occurred. A small group of Ioways had the opportunity to appear on an international stage. In 1844 fourteen men, women, and children traveled to Europe on a goodwill mission that they hoped would bring attention to their plight and, more important, raise money to help them pay their debts. In Europe the Ioways joined the painter and showman George Catlin for a tour of England, France, and Belgium as part of Catlin's "Indian Gallery" of paintings, artifacts, and live performances.

Catlin had known Ioway people for more than a decade. A native of Pennsylvania, he abandoned a career in law to follow his passion for art. By 1830 he had moved to St. Louis to specialize in painting portraits of America's Indigenous people. Catlin left St. Louis on the steamboat *Yellowstone* in March 1832 to embark on an eighteen-hundred-mile journey on the Missouri River. During that trip he created more than 135 paintings, many of which turned out to be the best of his long career. Along the way he visited the Ioways and noted that they were "the farthest departed from primitive modes" of all the tribes in the region. "They are depending chiefly on their cornfields for their substance," he reported, "though their appearance, both in their dwellings and personal looks . . . is that of the primitive Indian."[1]

Catlin's paintings and writings show that he was fascinated by the Ioways' "primitive" looks. In his *Letters and Notes on the North American Indians*, he boasted that his portraits of the Ioway warriors Shooting Cedar and Busy Man, captured them "tastefully dressed and equipped, the one with his war club on his arm, the other with bow and arrows in his hand; both wear around their waist beautiful buffalo robes and both had turbans of vari-colored cotton shawls, purchased of the Fur Traders. Around their necks were necklaces of the bear's claws, and a profusion of beads and wampum. Their ears were profusely strung with beads; their naked shoulders curiously streaked and daubed with red paint."[2]

In 1839 Catlin traveled to London with 507 of his paintings and opened an exhibition at the city's Egyptian Hall. There, surrounded by his artwork, the artist presented public programs about Native American culture. These programs included Catlin and other whites in Native costumes performing dances and reenacting battle scenes. As popular as the productions were, they attracted more attention when a group of Ojibwas joined the act in 1843. Catlin's relationship with the Ojibwas and their promoter, Arthur Rankin, was short-lived, however, and apparently ended unhappily in the spring of 1844.[3]

The Ioways left New York for Liverpool, England, on July, 1 1844, on a packet named the *Oxford*. The American writer Bayard Taylor, who was also a passenger aboard the *Oxford*, said that the Ioways helped relieve the tedium of the Atlantic voyage:

The chief [Francis White Cloud] was a very grave and dignified person, but some of the braves were merry enough. One day we had a war-dance on deck, which was a most ludicrous scene. The chief and two braves sat upon the deck, beating violently a small drum and howling forth their war-song, while the others in full dress, painted in a grotesque style, leaped about, brandishing tomahawks and spears, and terminating each dance with a terrific yell. Some of the men are very fine-looking, but the squaws are all ugly.[4]

In August the fourteen Ioways arrived in London with the promoter George Henry Curzon Melody. Catlin maintained that the Ioways' arrival was purely coincidental to his engaging them to perform and to tour Europe, but historian Joseph B. Herring has convincingly shown that plans for the Ioways' tour were laid before the tribe left the Great Nemaha Subagency. In fact Secretary of War J. M. Porter had personally agreed to allow the Ioways to make the trip and asked Francis White Cloud to select those who would travel with him. The party included White Cloud, his wife Rúúht^ánweMi (Strutting Pigeon Woman), and their daughter Sophia. Other Ioway leaders included Náx^ún Máñi (Hears Intermittently), who was also called the War Chief; Raining, who traveled with his ten-year-old son, the Commanding General; Always Dancing, whom Catlin called Jim; and the medicine man Blistered Feet, whom Catlin referred to as the Doctor. Little Wolf traveled with his wife, AkúweMi (She Herself Follows On), and their infant child Corsair (Pirate). White Cloud's old friend Jeffrey Deroine acted as the Ioways' translator on the trip.[5]

The newly arrived Ioways replaced the Ojibwas in a new series of shows at London's Egyptian Hall and later at Lord's Cricket Ground and Vauxhall Gardens. Melody and his occasional employer, circus showman P. T. Barnum, had previously tried to make money with programs that featured Indian actors, but they had failed. Observing that Catlin was a natural showman and that the Ioways trusted him, the pair contracted with the artist to handle the details of a European performance tour with the Ioways, for which Barnum provided financial backing.[6]

It is difficult to know whether it was White Cloud and the Ioways or the artist Catlin who initiated the Ioways' journey. Certainly, both parties had reasons for doing so. Ethnographer David Bernstein has proposed that the Ioways' trip to Europe was an attempt on their part to participate in the newly popular middle-class practice of leisure travel. Given the Io-ways' desperate state of poverty and the strong ties they still had to their own culture, this suggestion seems unlikely. However, Bernstein is more on target when he points out that the trip signified the Ioways' transition from the subsistence economy to the market economy. It does appear that White Cloud and his fellow travelers saw their participation in Catlin's pro-grams as an opportunity to make money. The Ioways were desperate to pay down the mounting debts they had accrued with traders. They were also hoping to use the trip to draw international attention to their dire situation at home. Their participation in Catlin's show is the first recorded example of Ioway people commoditizing elements of their culture. Ironi-cally, they performed rituals and dances that symbolized their former lives in the subsistence economy within the ticket-taking arena of the market economy. For the Ioways, the trade-off was simple. If offering their culture for hire in the form of performance made them participants in the market economy, it also offered a way out of their devastating cycle of poverty.[7]

Herring has suggested that there was a second reason that White Cloud and the other Ioways were interested in making the trip to Europe. Some hoped that the trip would enhance their standing with fellow tribal mem-bers at home. In past centuries tribal leaders routinely received medals, souvenirs, and articles of military clothing as gifts when meeting for treaty councils with colonial leaders from Spain, France, Britain, and the United States. Once home, headmen often found that these European articles en-hanced their status as tribal leaders. Given that government agents had been marginalizing the importance of Ioway leaders on the Great Nemaha Subagency, this scenario seems likely. White Cloud was especially eager to secure his standing as a strong and revered headman, and it seems en-tirely plausible that he hoped the opportunity to travel to Europe would enhance his status among his own people.[8]

Not everyone was pleased with the Ioways' travels to Europe, however. After the delegation had returned safely home, the Presbyterian mission-ary Samuel Irvin reported that he had initially been apprehensive about the trip. "We dreaded the result," Irvin confided in a letter to Catlin in 1847. "So far as our opinion was consulted, it was given against the design, advising rather that they should stay at home, go to labor and economy, and not go to be shown as wild animals." Irvin worried that, once away from home, the Ioways would be vulnerable to influences of "bad company" and would engage in excessive drinking on their travels. He was also concerned about the "probability of their going to France, and becoming enchanted with the externals of the Catholic religion."[9]

Catlin noted that during the Ioways' first performance before a small group of his friends, "their very appearance, as they entered the room, was so wild and classic, that it brought forth applause from every part of the hall." The artist's guests delighted in the Ioways and declared that they were "altogether more primitive in their appearance and modes, and decidedly a finer body of men" than the Ojibwas. The Ioways thrilled the crowd with two dances that Catlin described as an Eagle dance and a Warrior's dance. Subsequent performances included a Bear dance and a Scalp dance, which Catlin pointed out, was performed with genuine human scalps.[10]

Some critics, including Charles Dickens, denounced Catlin for exploiting the Ioways, but Catlin maintained they had approached him about participating in the programs. "They had come a great way, and with a view to make something to carry home to their women and children," Catlin wrote. "I was in hopes that my efforts might aid in enabling them to do so." While this is probably not entirely accurate, it does seem clear that White Cloud and the other Ioways willingly participated in the programs and that Catlin gave them the freedom to choose which rituals and dances they would perform.[11]

In early 1845 Catlin moved his show to Paris where the Ioways had an audience with King Louis-Philippe and attracted the attention of many among the city's wealthy and cultural elite. As Herring has noted, however, the attention the Ioways garnered was not always the kind of attention they had hoped for. While France's royal family lavished them with medals and gifts and hundreds attended their shows, the French public was drawn more by the prospect of seeing authentic untamed American aborigines than by concern for the poverty and hardship that plagued them and their relatives in United States. Even the French writer George Sand, who had been an advocate for Europe's disenfranchised underclass and who interviewed the Ioways and wrote an article about them, was more attracted to the way they embodied the myth of the Noble Savage than to their status as some of America's poorest and most impoverished people.[12]

George Catlin and His Troupe of Iowa Performing in the Tuileries before Louis-Philippe and His Family, 1845 (oil on canvas). Karl Girardet (1813–71). King Louis-Philippe, Queen Marie-Amélie, and the duchess of Orleans attending a dance by Iowa Natives in the Salon de la Paix at the Tuileries, presented by the painter George Catlin on April 21, 1845. During their travels in Europe with Catlin, fourteen Ioways performed traditional dances and songs for the public and royalty alike. (© RMN-Grand Palais / Art Resource, NY.)

In the end the financial assistance the Ioways had hoped would help them pay their debts at home never materialized. By the time Catlin moved his Indian Gallery to Paris, Barnum and Melody had withdrawn their support, and the artist found it increasingly difficult to manage the show on his own. While the Ioways talked with many Europeans about the state of their poverty and asked many for help, no benefactors stepped forward with offers to assist them financially. Instead many offered to convert them to Christianity, believing that through their salvation, the Ioways might become "civilized" and their difficulties would be ended. Given this interest in saving the Ioways' souls it is not surprising that, while the Ioways did not benefit financially from the trip, the Presbyterian Mission at the Great Nemaha Subagency did. Missions in Europe sent aid to the Presbyterians. "Very important pecuniary aid, both in money and clothing, was . . . received, from which our cause has in no small degree, been aided and encouraged," reported Irvin. He also noted that one man whom the Ioways met in England, Paul Bloohm, was so taken with them that he followed them home and became a Presbyterian missionary.[13]

In the end the trip was more than a disappointment for the Ioways. Three of them—the War Chief, AkúweMi, and the young Corsair—died in Europe. When the remaining Ioways returned to the United States in the fall of 1845, they brought home hundreds of worthless trinkets and medals, 105 Bibles, and very little money. However, the trip may not have been without its benefits. Herring has argued that the Ioways' travels did provide them with a better understanding of European American culture. While their tour had greatly raised the Ioways' profile in the cities of Europe, Francis White Cloud and the other delegates quickly realized that their celebrity status meant little to the settlers and politicians of western Missouri. While Catlin and their Europeans hosts had seen the Ioways as untamed children of the wilderness, the Ioways' European American neighbors held no such romantic views. To them the Ioways were simply an impediment that prevented them from settling the farmland of eastern Kansas.

In order to survive in the hostile situation in which they found themselves at home, the Ioways realized they had to adapt. Herring contends that their European tour made Ioway leaders "even more determined to build a more secure future for" their people. Their strategy, writes Herring, "was to become as unobtrusive as possible and, therefore, less of a threat to their white neighbors." Roy W. Meyer and David Bernstein have both suggested that the "secure future" the Ioways were seeking involved the adaption of certain elements of a European American culture, primarily agriculture.[14] While this is true, agriculture was just one of several elements the Ioways used to adapt to the white world.

The rationale for moving the Ioways, Sacs, and Foxes west of the Missouri River in 1836 had been to separate them from the land-hungry settlers who had been the source of so much conflict in the Platte Country located between Missouri's old western border and the Missouri River. The language of the Treaty of 1836 had been crafted in such a way as to force the Ioways to concede that any attempt on their part to use the ceded lands "must inevitably lead to collisions with citizens of the United States."[15] For a time this strategy worked, and settlers generally stayed on the Missouri side of the river.

But soon the pressure of westward expansion brought settlers across the river onto the Ioways' new land. Many came via the Oregon Trail, a popular route with settlers traveling west in the early 1840s. By the time Francis White Cloud and his fellow travelers returned from Europe in 1846, emigrants had discovered that, by fording the Missouri River at St. Joseph, Missouri, rather than farther south at Independence, Missouri, they could shorten their journey by a hundred miles and by several days. The discovery transformed the sleepy village of St. Joseph into a boomtown seemingly overnight. This boom helped St. Joseph reach a population of about one thousand by 1846. The community sustained another jump in population after a mill foreman named James Marshall discovered traces of gold in a stream near John Sutter's mill in California's central valley in January 1848. Just over a year later more than twenty-five hundred wagons crossed the Missouri River from the St. Joseph area in a ten-week period and an estimated total of fifty thousand people passed through the city during the 1849 calendar year. Much to the chagrin of the Ioways, the preferred route of most of the travelers who crossed the river at St. Joseph cut through the southern portion of the Great Nemaha Subagency.[16]

The most commonly used trail route passed within a few hundred feet of the mission school and agency buildings. That roadway brought not only people to the subagency but livestock as well. Just one caravan, which passed through on May 17, 1844, included 323 people riding in 72 wagons. Trailing the caravan were 713 horned cattle, 54 horses, and 41 mules. Such heavy traffic took a heavy toll on the land. Settlers cut wood for cooking fires, and the livestock ate large quantities of grass and even the Ioways' crops. Emigrant trains also brought disease, primarily cholera, to the subagency's inhabitants. In May 1849, the *St. Joseph Gazette* reported that wagons on the Great Nemaha Subagency stretched "as far as the eye could see."[17]

For many emigrants, crossing the Missouri River meant leaving the United States and entering the unknown of Indian Territory in which many expected to suffer at the hands of "savage Indians." For the most part, however, contact between travelers and Natives were free of conflict. Emigrants were intrigued by the appearance of the first Native people many of them had ever seen. Several remembered the Natives' ubiquitous red-and-green blankets, which they seemed to keep wrapped around them at all time in all weather. Sarah Sutton recalled more specific details about their dress: "Several [Natives] came to see us, their heads were shaved all but a narrow strip from the crown of their head back and that stood strait up, and their head and temples painted red, and they wore heavy ear rings, and beads on their necks and rings on their wrists. I think they were fixed in their Sunday best, to see the Emigrants, and get all they could of them."[18]

Traveler Sarah Davis noted that her party had a "very bad time with the Indians," while on the trail in May 1850. She recorded one encounter with a Native man who rode up to them on his horse and told them to get off his land and go home. Davis and her party of emigrants felt threatened by the man, in large part because he was intoxicated, but the settlers managed to end the encounter without a struggle. Under these circumstances, many travelers found the mission to be "a cheerful site in this wild region" and sometimes lingered within view of its houses, barns, fences, and fields before venturing to the uncertainty that awaited them farther west.[19]

While the Ioways, Sacs, and Foxes inflicted little harm on the settlers, the trail and those who followed it brought harm to the Natives and inflicted damage on the land on which they lived. Among some Ioways, oral tradition persists suggesting that Native people, especially girls and young women, disappeared during the years that emigrant traffic passed through the subagency. Some Ioways recall hearing stories that claimed white emigrants took young Ioway women from the subagency and forced them to help with domestic chores such as cooking and childcare.[20] St. Joseph folklorist Mary Alicia Owen heard similar stories during the many trips she made to visit the Ioways, Sacs, and Foxes in the 1880s and 1890s. Owen published a book about the folklore of the Sacs and Foxes in 1904 and later published two versions of a story about a Native girl stolen from the subagency by settlers. In a version of the tale she called "Poor Lucy," written sometime between 1910 and 1920, a family of settlers named Blackwell passed through the subagency in the spring of 1849 on their way to the

California fields. Spying some Native children picking wild strawberries, they lured one girl into their wagon with a piece of gingerbread. "Without a thought to what that squaw's kin would do to the next train," wrote Owen, "they kept the little girl for a playmate for their child and carried her to California." Returning two years later, "draggle-tailed and discouraged" by their failure to strike it rich, the Blackwells leave the girl, whom they named Lucy, near the spot where they had found her. In the years that followed, the girl was driven insane by her inability to relocate her birth family who had moved away during her absence.[21]

The Ioways also endured vandalism caused by curious souvenir hunters passing through their land. During the 1840s the Ioways still practiced scaffold internment of their dead. These remains proved highly visible curiosities that many travelers mentioned in their diaries. Camping near Mosquito Creek, seven miles east of the mission, in the spring of 1847, settler C. W. Cooke noted "an old Indian warrior wrapped in his rug, and sitting high up in an oak tree was a striking example of the peculiar mode of interment." Two years later traveler Vincent Geiger saw a coffin containing the remains of "an old Indian Chief who died about four years ago" in a tree near Spider Creek. Despite the fact that he judged the coffin to be thirty feet above the ground, he could not resist taking a bead from it. Given the broad acceptance of taking souvenirs from Native remains during the nineteenth century, it is highly likely that many travelers saw no harm in doing as Geiger had done.[22]

The Ioways used more than one means to receive compensation for the heavy toll Oregon Trail emigrants exacted on their land and their people. By the late 1840s they had begun to appeal directly to travelers to pay them for the damage they were causing. Two days journey west of St. Joseph, emigrants encountered the Wolf River, an obstacle many had difficulty crossing. As the river crossing was on the Ioways' land, members of the tribe began asking travelers to pay them a toll. On one occasion in June 1849 James Hutchens paid a small group of Ioway men a toll of fifty cents to cross the river. In return Hutchens asked the Ioways to help his party across. They made a good show of pushing the wagon through the riverbed but the load proved too heavy, and they had to unpack the wagon and carry their provisions across by hand.[23]

By 1850 the Ioways had constructed a wooden bridge over the crossing. A traveler named James Hawkins Clark, who days earlier had paid five dollars to cross the Missouri River at St. Joseph, complained bitterly about having to pay the Ioways one dollar to cross a fifty-foot-long bridge that, in his estimation, cost $150 dollars to build. The toll takers would not accept gold pieces, asking instead to be paid in "white money with a bird on it," which further incensed the traveler who grumbled, "California should be full of gold if the immigrant expects to get back all his outlay for getting there." Travelers reported paying anywhere from twenty-five cents to one dollar to cross the Ioways' toll bridge. If estimates that claim fourteen hundred wagons had crossed the new bridge by May 9, 1850, the Ioways' made a fair amount of money from the enterprise. Some travelers refused to pay to cross the creek, a few even going as far as building their own crude spans, but most paid the toll fearing, as emigrant Sarah Sutton wrote, that it "would make war with the Indians" if they did not.[24]

If travelers expected to pass freely after crossing the bridge, they were disappointed. Sacs and Foxes, who apparently did not share in the Ioways profits, asked travelers to pay them a toll as well. Some settlers reported that those who asked them for compensation carried papers signed by their subagent stating that they were doing so with his consent. While some complied with the request others, like Osborn Cross, refused. A Sac man approached his party and asked for a "small present" for the wood they had burned and the grass their cattle had eaten. Cross fed the man and sent him away without cash compensation. "If these people really deserved compensation," he wrote, "which was of itself too absurd to think of for a moment, it was a proper subject to lay before the Indian department."[25]

In a council with Subagent Richardson in January 1850, the Ioways did just that. The headman No Heart outlined the devastating effect these travelers had on the subagency. "They travel through here every year and last spring there were thousands of men, wagons and oxen went through. They drank our water, ate our grass, burnt our timber, and what is worse brought a bad sickness (cholera) among us which killed many of our people, making us very sorry." To help pay for the damages the travelers had caused, No Heart shrewdly told Richardson he wanted his "Great Father to add at least five hundred dollars a year to our annuities to pay for this. This will make our hearts glad and make the road wider for other white people." Three years later Superintendent of Indian Affairs in St. Louis

David Mitchell recommended to Commissioner of Indian Affairs Luke Lea that money be paid to the Ioways, Sacs, and Foxes to cover damages that emigrants had done to crops in their fields.[26]

The Ioways received some satisfaction from the payments they received as compensation for damage along the trail route, but another larger difficulty soon developed involving land. As early as October 1851 the few settlers living in the unincorporated Nebraska Territory, west of the states of Missouri and Iowa, began to urge Congress to establish a "regular territorial government." The number of these settlers was small because the land that would make up Kansas and Nebraska had been set aside exclusively for Native people. Indian agents, missionaries, and licensed traders were the only white people legally allowed to live on the land. Others living in the region were technically squatters. Although few in number this constituency soon found it had powerful allies in the nation's capital. The Mexican war, which ended in 1848, had opened California to settlers. Politicians, railroad magnates, and other businessmen began to view the Indian land between the Missouri River and the west coast as a barrier to the expansion of the United States.[27]

To organize the region Illinois senator Stephen A. Douglas led the effort in 1853 to draft legislation that would create two new territories of Kansas and Nebraska west of the Missouri River. Passing the bill, which became known as the Kansas-Nebraska Act, proved fraught with difficulty. The main political sticking point revolved around the question of whether slavery would be allowed in the new territories. The Missouri Compromise of 1820 had forbidden slavery in any new state or territory located north of the 36°30′ latitude. Since both the proposed territories of Kansas and Nebraska were north of that line, the compromise would have banned slavery within their borders. To win the votes of Southern congressmen who were reluctant to create two new free territories, Douglas promoted the concept of popular, or squatter, sovereignty. Popular sovereignty allowed settlers of the new territories to decide for themselves whether they would become free states or slave states.

Congress passed the Kansas-Nebraska Act on May 26, 1854, and it became law just four days later. By May 27, thousands—one witness estimated as many as thirty thousand—of settlers were waiting along Missouri's western border to stake land claims in the new Kansas Territory. Unfortunately when these settlers flooded across the border, there was no land legally available in the new territory for them to claim. The government had begun to negotiate land cessions with most of the Native nations living in eastern Kansas, but the U.S. Senate had not yet ratified any of the resulting treaties. Just two weeks before the Kansas-Nebraska Act took effect, the Ioways, Sacs, and Foxes had signed treaties that cut the size of their combined land from four hundred square miles to about one hundred square miles. This and similar treaties in the region were designed to open up land for settlement, yet treaty provisions prohibited settlers from claiming the ceded land until after a government land survey was complete. None of this deterred the settlers, however. By June 26, 1854, settlers had claimed most of the land the Ioways, Sacs, and Foxes had just ceded near the Great Nemaha Agency.[28]

Prior to the Kansas-Nebraska Act, the U.S. government had tended to follow an orderly process by which it made ceded Indian land available to settlers. Generally that process began with the government entering into a treaty in which a Native nation ceded or sold rights to land it claimed. Once the treaty was ratified by the U.S. Senate, the General Land Office would conduct a survey of the land, dividing it into square-mile, 640-acre sections. Once surveyed the land was then offered to the public at auction. Only then was it legal for settlers to occupy or claim the land. Because eager settlers often staked out claims before the prescribed process was complete, Congress passed a law of preemption, which recognized the rights of squatters in 1841.[29]

In Kansas, however, these normal procedures were thrown aside as politicians and business interests hoped to accommodate quick settlement of the new territory. This particular land rush was not only motivated by the natural push of westward expansion, it was also fueled by political ideology related to the issue of slavery. Because the provision of popular sovereignty had been written into the Kansas-Nebraska Act, both proslavery and abolitionist organizations from other parts of the country rushed to send groups of settlers into the new territory in hopes of influencing the outcome of the territory's eventual vote on the question of slavery. Railroad interests were also eager to enter the new territory in order to establish routes for a transcontinental line that would persuade the government to grant them land and loans.[30]

As settlers flooded into the new territory the Ioways began their retreat north toward the Great Nemaha River and the remaining sections of land they still possessed. Although their agency had been greatly diminished the Ioways were, in a sense, fortunate to have retained any land in the Kansas Territory. Herring has argued that the Ioways, Sacs, Foxes, and other nations were able to remain in Kansas by carefully walking "the line between their traditional ways and those of the whites," by acculturating rather than assimilating to European American society. According to Herring, the Indigenous people who remained in Kansas may have learned to speak English and begun farming and dressing like whites but they never forgot their kinship, customs, or religion. By successfully navigating this line they made themselves less threatening and more outwardly acceptable to their new white neighbors.[31]

Roy W. Meyer and David Bernstein have both argued that the Ioways in particular accomplished this by practicing European American methods of agriculture. Four years after they signed the Treaty of 1854, the Ioways were farming 250 acres of corn, wheat, oats, beans, pumpkins, and potatoes. By 1859 they had increased their cultivated acreage to six hundred acres. By the time John A. Burbank succeeded Vanderslice as the Great Nemaha agent in 1861, the Ioways were beginning to make the transition toward farming individual plots of land and asking the agent for help in building European American style houses.[32]

Newspaper accounts from the period tell a slightly different story, however. Although whites living near the agency did not generally perceive the Ioways as a threat, they had a hard time accepting them as anything other than stereotypical Indians. In 1857 seven investors—including Richard Gatling, the inventor of the Gatling gun—pooled their money to plat the town of White Cloud along the Missouri River, just east of the newly downsized agency. That same year Sol Miller began publishing the *White Cloud Kansas Chief*. Anecdotes featuring the often humorous exploits of Ioways appeared in the pages of Miller's paper. Under headlines such as "Great Time Among the Indians—Heap Dog!" or "Indian Shin-Dig," Miller printed stories that played upon picturesque scenes of "half-naked rascals" and "graceful Indian women," singing and dancing. He also pointed out instances of what to him seemed to be the Natives' inscrutable behavior. For instance, he wondered why a group of Natives would purchase one lot of sleigh bells from a White Cloud store. "What they wanted with them, except . . . to hear them tinkle, is more than we can 'reckon,'" Miller wrote. "They never enjoy the luxury of sleigh riding."[33]

While whites enjoyed making light of the Natives' behavior, they also held a number of darker negative stereotypes about their Native neighbors. Most prevalent among these was the belief that all Indians were drunks. "I never saw an Indian in my life but what liked whiskey," stated an area resident named James Dyche. As we have seen, alcohol was a problem at the agency and it led to fights and the deaths of many Ioways. But, as Miller reasoned, "If the Indians quarreled only among themselves, it would not concern the whites so much." Whites feared alcohol-related violence involving Natives, especially when it took place in the streets of White Cloud and on nearby farmsteads, because it constituted a threat to their sense of security. While this nurtured white prejudice against the Ioways, Sacs, and Foxes, it also led whites to pressure whiskey traders to cease their "doggery business" or at least to move it elsewhere.[34]

Some settlers living near the agency also held the stereotypical belief that Native women were promiscuous or "loose." This was due in no small measure to the way in which Ioway traditions of marriage differed from those of the whites. While Ioways did have marriage ceremonies they did not resemble those of the Christian-style weddings. As Mahecomi (also known as Mrs. Wilson), an Ioway woman living on the agency at the time, explained, when an Ioway couple considered living together, "they talked to one another and if they liked one another, [the man] took the girl home to his people and gave presents to the girl's parents . . . if they did not get along, they just quit living together, and went to live with someone else."[35]

This led to the perception among whites that Ioway women were routinely bought and sold like prostitutes and had no moral grounding. This misperception was further supported by the fact that the daughters of some well-to-do Ioways wore tattoos on their faces. While these tattoos were marks of distinction rendered during ceremony by an esteemed member of the women's clan, whites believed the marks denoted those who were "not a right kind of woman." In fact Ioway women were sometimes engaged as prostitutes in St. Joseph and White Cloud. In at least one case, however, white whiskey traders exploited the women for the benefit of white customers.[36]

Even though such stereotypes led many whites to distance themselves from their Ioway neighbors, the Ioways were determined to stay in the area. Their success in retaining a portion of their agency was due in part to their willingness to play a more engaged game of give-and-take with the U.S. government then they had in previous treaty negotiations. White Cloud, who had often sparred with government officials, died in December 1851. This left the more flexible No Heart as the Ioways' lead negotiator for the Treaty of 1854. The Ioway delegates, which also included Little Wolf, British, and The Man Who Steals, expressed their readiness to sell some of the Ioways' land to the United States, but they steadfastly refused to consider selling it all. They recalled that when they had been forced to move west of the Missouri River in 1837, the government had promised the Ioways that the agency would be their final home. When the government asked them to move once again, the Ioways said no and Commissioner of Indian Affairs George Manypenny lacked the political heart to force their removal.[37]

In the years leading up to the treaty, the Ioways had actively discussed various options for remaining at their current homeland with Agent Vanderslice and with the Presbyterian missionaries. One idea they entertained called for allotting quarter-section (160-acre) parcels of agency land to individual Ioways. Once these plots had been assigned, all "extra" land surrounding the Ioway allotments would be sold to settlers. Allotment was part of Vanderslice's plan to civilize the Ioways. By breaking up the Ioways' communal land, scattering them from their villages, and by forcing them to abandon their traditional clothing for "citizens clothes," the agent believed he could make great strides in turning his charges into subsistence farmers. Vanderslice believed that life among settlers would help the Ioways assimilate more quickly into the dominant white society.[38]

While Commissioner Manypenny believed that the future of the Ioways and other Native people in Kansas rested in their eventual settlement on individual allotments, he worried that the onslaught of settlers would prove too destructive and harmful. "Trespasses and depredations of every conceivable kind have been committed on the Indian," he wrote. "They have been personally maltreated, their property stolen, their timber destroyed[,] their possessions encroached upon and diverse other injuries done them." Samuel Irvin, the Presbyterian missionary, agreed that allowing settlers to claim land among Ioway allotments would lead to trouble. He maintained that the plan did not "afford any better prospect of advantage to the Indian. He would be instantly imposed upon, and likely find redress, for wrongs endured, not easily obtained."[39]

Throughout the discussions the Ioways let it be known that they preferred to retain a communal parcel of land rather than accept allotments.
Irvin hinted that it was the Ioways who, in 1852, first introduced the idea
of retaining a small centralized agency of about one hundred square miles.
As they departed for Washington and the treaty negotiations on April 19,
1854, the four Ioway delegates remained determined to retain at least a
portion of that land. They also expressed a willingness to forgo their future
annuities if the government would pay them all of the money it held in
trust for them. With that money in hand the Ioways believed they could
pay their debts, support a school, and invest in their future needs.[40]

The final treaty was signed on May 17, 1854, and shows that the Ioways
were partially successful. They retained approximately one-fourth of their
reservation land. The victory was not without compromise, however. While
some, including the missionaries, hoped that the boundaries of the new
reservation would include the mission, the agency buildings, and the Sac
farm, the final plan moved the Ioways approximately eight miles north,
presumably to clear the route of the Oregon Trail and any subsequent rail
lines that might follow in its wake. While the Ioways received money to
build new homes, purchase agricultural implements, and make improvements on new fields, the government refused to let them use trust money
to pay their individual debts. During the treaty negotiations the government also elicited a promise from the Ioways to devote themselves to "in-
dustry, thrift and morality," and to renew their efforts to abstain from
alcohol.[41]

Throughout the negotiations government representatives held on to the
hope that the Ioways would eventually accept allotment. In a provision
that was to predate the Dawes Act by thirty-three years, the treaty gave the
president of the United States the discretion to order the Ioways' land to
be surveyed at the Ioways' expense and allotted to individual heads of
household. In September, as the Ioways were preparing to move to their
new land, Vanderslice met in full council with them and asked them to
disband their village and to settle on individual allotments across the reservation. "If this rule can be strictly enforced and continued, their condition will have begun to improve. . . . Fewer [Indians] being together, there
will be less inducement to idleness, drinking, gambling, and other low and
groveling debaucheries."[42]

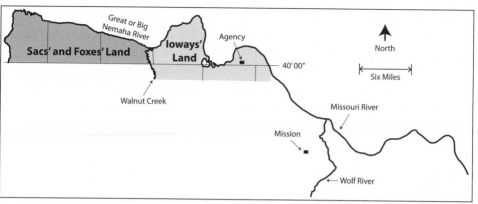

The boundaries of the Great Nemaha Agency, 1854–61. (Map by the author. Copyright © 2016, University of Oklahoma Press.)

Talk of allotment was delayed, however, as more pressing complexities of the agency move became apparent, and the rush of settlers to claim the newly ceded land commenced. By early November all but two Ioway families had completed the short move to the new land. In December Vanderslice complained that they had settled too close together and that it took his "continual exertion to break up their village system." He admitted, however, that the Ioways were "certainly trying to do better than heretofore." The Sacs and Foxes were waiting for their portion of the new agency to be surveyed and had not yet begun to relocate. The Ioways, Sacs, and Foxes had all reminded Agent Vanderslice that they expected money to aid them in their resettlement. The agent could only tell them that the funds, which were dependent on the speed of their removal, would be forthcoming.[43]

While the survey of the new reservation proceeded according to plan, problems quickly arose in making a survey of the ceded agency land. Isaac McCoy's 1837 survey of the original Great Nemaha Subagency boundaries had been so hastily completed that the Bureau of Indian Affairs had difficulty locating a copy of his field notes. While Vanderslice consulted with the bureau's main office in Washington and struggled to reconstruct the survey, settlers grew anxious about the distribution of the new land. Citing the Preemption Law of 1841 settlers began to claim parcels of the Ioway cession, even though U.S. Attorney General Caleb Cushing had ruled that allowing preemption would be "a violation of the treaties, a breach of trust, a fraud upon the Indians."[44]

The agent had been able to prevent some from squatting on the Ioway cession but had not been able to keep others from settling on the Sac cession east of the Wolf River. Although Vanderslice had distributed handbills and published a notice in the *St. Joseph Gazette* reminding settlers that it was illegal to occupy Indian land, these had proved ineffective. The attorney general's ruling notwithstanding, most settlers believed that the government would never resort to forcibly removing squatters from their claims. The agent believed that the squatters' associations had emboldened settlers to defy the government's warning, and over the next three years he routinely pleaded with Superintendent of Indian Affairs Alfred Cummings to authorize the use of troops to remove squatters. He described the situation as a "mania pervading throughout the country," adding that "Men, who in everything else, seem to be prudent run wild in their efforts to accumulation of lands."[45]

Squatters' associations were "extra-legal" groups of settlers who banded together to record claims, enforce self-imposed rules, and settle claim disputes among members. Although he complained about them Vanderslice, along with his son Thomas, belonged to and benefited from membership in a squatters' association in the so-called Whitehead district. Named after James R. Whitehead, a trader who established a settlement across the Missouri River from St. Joseph, Missouri, the district encompassed agency land that was to be opened to settlement as part of the Treaty of 1854. In all, 136 settlers registered claims with the group.[46]

Meanwhile William Banks, the prominent settler from Holt County, Missouri, who operated a ferry, hemp warehouse, and store at Iowa Point, became alarmed when he heard rumors that Ioway headmen were agreeing to sell land directly to settlers. He wrote to Commissioner of Indian Affairs Manypenny to express his concern that unscrupulous land speculators would persuade some Ioways to sell them land for "a horse or two." He asked the commissioner to be vigilant in ensuring the Ioways' ceded land be sold by public auction. As the process of making the lands available for the public became drawn out, he worried that the government's lack of progress would result in a decrease in the land's value. In a second letter to Manypenny in 1856, he pointed out that settlers were stripping much of the Ioway cession of its valuable timber.[47]

Finally, in June 1857, the land the Ioways had ceded three years earlier was sold to the public. Contrary to the treaty, however, the Bureau of Indian Affairs allowed most of the land to be sold directly to the squatters for appraised prices that ranged between $1.75 and $2.75 per acre. In May Commissioner I. W. Denver had warned Norman Eddy, the special commissioner appointed to oversee the land sale, that the bureau would have "no sympathy" for land speculators who might try to buy land at public auction without paying for improvements squatters had made while living on it. He instructed Eddy to allow land sales to squatters whenever their claims could be validated. Vanderslice reported that more than ninety-four thousand acres of land sold for a total of $184,000, or slightly less than two dollars an acre—about half the land's fair market value. Despite the bureau's attempt to validate all claims, as soon as the sale was complete more than one-third of the settlers transferred their tracts directly to land speculators for whom they had been holding the land. In the end the bureau had not only been unable to keep the big money interests out, they had deprived the Ioways the opportunity to get the full market value for their ceded land.[48]

The Ioways asked that they be allowed to send a delegation to Washington where they planned to request an immediate payment of $30,000 from the proceeds of the sale. The three years following the Treaty of 1854 had been difficult ones of the Ioways. In their efforts to relocate and expand their farming operation, they had accumulated a significant debt to traders. Vanderslice estimated that they owed one trader between $5,000 and $6,000—equal to approximately a quarter of a million dollars today. The Ioways had not received an annuity payment in two years and according to Vanderslice they had "become destitute and of clothing and their usual means of subsistence." On the agent's advice the Bureau of Indian Affairs refused to receive a delegation of Ioways in Washington, but they did agree to make a payment of $20,460—or $47.25 per person—to the Ioways.[49]

In the meantime Ioway leaders and Agent Vanderslice had once again begun to discuss the possibility of Ioways living on individual plots of land. Ioway leaders asked their agent to make arrangements to have their land surveyed "so that those [Ioways] selecting homesteads may have a property in the tract with the boundaries designated." Vanderslice wholeheartedly endorsed the idea as a "means of improving their condition." He did recommend that, if the Ioways received homesteads, the land be held in trust so that individuals could not sell their property "for at least many years." The Ioways' move must have greatly encouraged Vanderslice, who had noticed other changes in the Ioways in the years after their 1854 relocation. In January 1856 he reported that many of the Ioway headmen had appeared at a council wearing "citizen's clothes." They told Vanderslice that they wore them because they wanted to become "White Men in habit." In that same meeting they had also expressed their desire to acquire more plows and wagons and wanted the government to build them additional houses.[50]

By 1858, however, the Ioways were once again defending their reservation land from settlers. Rumors had it that the Ioways, Sacs, and Foxes would soon sign another treaty with the U.S. government and more reservation land would be available to settlers. The *White Cloud Kansas Chief* proclaimed, "The Iowa and Sac Reservations are in the possession of these tribes. There has been no treaty, nor is there a prospect of any, by which the Indian title will be extinguished; and the Government is bound to protect the Indians in their rights." Agent Vanderslice placed a notice in the *Chief* warning all trespassers on reservation land that he would be forced to "put in force the laws of the United States," against them.[51]

This warning did not stop white settlers from trespassing on Indian land to steal timber. In January 1860 Vanderslice complained about the problem to his new supervisor, Superintendent of Indian Affairs in St. Joseph A. M. Robinson. "The reservations of the Sacs and Foxes and of the Iowas are surrounded by the settlements of the whites and their towns," the agent explained. "The Indians in selecting their reservations have incorporated within their boundaries much of the best timber land in all this section of the country, hence unscrupulous persons have settled on prairie lands contiguous to the reserve, hoping to make their improvements from Indian timber."[52]

For several days Vanderslice braved winter cold and snow to travel the country in an attempt to ascertain the extent of the problem. He saw ample evidence of cut timber and spoke with several settlers who admitted taking trees, but he was forced to let them go with a warning. He did not have the manpower to arrest the perpetrators and did not have a place to hold them for trial, nor was there any court nearby to hear the cases. In

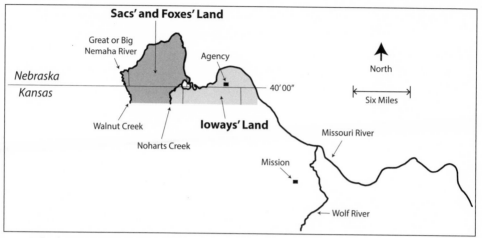

The boundaries of the Great Nemaha Agency, 1861. (Map by the author. Copyright © 2016, University of Oklahoma Press.)

order to help relieve the situation, Vanderslice was allowed to hire Harvey W. Foreman, the Sacs' and Foxes' farmer, to "watch over the Sac and Foxes of Missouri and protect them and their property and especially their timber from the depredations of whites."[53]

This set the stage for yet another Ioways' land cession in 1861. On March 6 Vanderslice assembled the Ioways and the Sac and Fox in a joint council on the Great Nemaha Agency. He persuaded the Sacs and Foxes to relinquish all that remained of their reservation, some thirty-two thousand acres. He then convinced the Ioways to give up half of what remained of their reservation for the Sacs and Foxes. The terms were similar to those spelled out in the Treaty of 1854. The Sacs' and Foxes' land would be sold at public auction, and the proceeds from the sale would be split between the two tribes. Half would be paid to them directly and the government would hold half in trust. The interest from that trust was to be paid out to the tribes as part of the annual annuity payment.[54]

The Treaty of 1861 would be the last between the United States and the Ioway people. A decade later the federal government would cease conducting treaties with Indian nations and the long trail of Ioways' land cession treaties that had begun in 1824 would end. The story of the Ioways and their land would not end there, however. By 1878 some Ioways who were dissatisfied with life in Kansas had begun to migrate to the Indian Territory to live with members of the Sac and Fox nation. In 1883 the Ioways were granted their own reservation in the Indian Territory, now known as Oklahoma. A decade later that land—as well as the land at the Great Nemaha Agency—was allotted to the Ioway people as part of the Dawes Act.

Conclusion

Long, long ago, the Ioways were bears, elk, buffalo, wolves, beavers, eagles . . . then there was change and those Ioways became humans, they lost their fur, their horns, their wings, their claws and became Indians. Not having horns or wings or claws did not stop them from being Ioways.

Not so long ago, there was further change, and those Ioway Indians transformed again, and most lost their braids, their shiny black hair, their coppery skin and flint eyes. Now through that change we are still Ioways, but our skins are often pale, eyes blue or green, our hair red, blonde or brown.

Lance Foster (Ioway)

The Ioways were able to resist many of the changes that government agents and Presbyterian missionaries tried to force on them during their first two decades on the Great Nemaha Agency.[1] While the Ioways lost a significant amount of control over the manner in which they governed themselves and their ability to provide for their own economic well-being, they did manage to retain many of their spiritual and cultural traditions. They also succeeded in retaining a foothold in the new state of Kansas. Nonetheless, in the more than 150 years since the story chronicled in this book took place, the Ioway people have changed considerably. One thing that remains is their connection to the land that was once a part of the Great Nemaha Agency. Land use, land rights, and land stewardship continued to play a major role in the history of the Ioways after 1860, and land remains a big part of the Ioways' lives today.

At least one piece of legal business related to the Treaty of 1854 and the 1857 sale of the Ioways' ceded portion of the Great Nemaha Agency remained unsettled for more than a century. In 1969 the Indian Claims Commission ruled that the United States had "breached its duty to the Iowa[y] Tribe" in the way it mishandled the sale of Ioway land. By allowing squatters to purchase land they had preemptively claimed at its appraised price, the government denied the Ioways the opportunity to receive the full market value they could have expected had the land been sold at public auction as was directed by the Treaty of 1854. Because of this the commission found that in 1857 the Ioways were cheated out of more than $193,000. Adjusted for inflation, this amount was roughly equal to $759,000 in 1969. The commission further found that the Ioways had been defrauded of an additional $14,000 in 1855, because they had not been compensated for land they allowed the Sacs and Foxes to use after the agency was relocated to the bluffs overlooking the Great Nemaha River. With interest, the commission ruled that the government owed the Ioways $1.36 million.[2]

In the meantime many Ioways left the Great Nemaha Agency to a new home farther south. During the 1860s and 1870s efforts had continued to disband the agency. With the opening of the Indian Territory, now known as Oklahoma, white settlers made a number of unsuccessful attempts to persuade the government to uproot all Native people living in Kansas and move them there. After the Civil War some Sacs and Foxes did relocate to the Indian Territory and encouraged their former Ioway neighbors to join them.

In 1877 the Ioways held a referendum to decide whether to send a delegation to the south for the purpose of scouting out locations for a new home in the Indian Territory. After a split vote the Ioways officially dropped the idea. The following year, however, some Ioways decided that they wanted to move south to live among the Sacs and Foxes. Over time more followed, and by the end of 1879 there were about fifty Ioways living on the Sac and Fox reservation. On August 15, 1883, the Ioways received 228,418 acres of Sac and Fox land for their own reservation. By that time the total population of Ioways had dwindled to only about two hundred. Slightly less than half of them lived on the new reservation.[3]

Those Ioways who moved south in the 1870s and 1880s are now officially recognized as the Iowa Tribe of Oklahoma. Their tribal offices are located south of Perkins, Oklahoma, near the Cimarron River. Through the Dawes Act the government allotted land on the reservation to enrolled members in 1890. By 2011 the tribe had a total enrollment of 697 members, and over 500 lived in Oklahoma.[4] The tribal government provides social services for its residents and operates a smoke shop, convenience store, art gallery, and casino. The southern Ioways, as they are sometimes called, are also engaged in a number of cultural and language preservation programs.

Despite subsequent attempts to disband the Ioways' reservation along the Great Nemaha River the Iowa Tribe of Kansas and Nebraska, or northern Ioways, remain in that location today. While there were barely 100 northern Ioways on the rolls in the 1880s, there were 2,880 enrolled members of the Iowa Tribe of Kansas and Nebraska in 2004. Only about 500 of those, however, live on or near the reservation. The land on this reservation too was allotted to tribal members through the Dawes Act in 1891.[5] The boundaries of the Ioway's reservation in Kansas and Nebraska have remained mostly unchanged since 1861, but much of the land inside those boundaries has been lost as individual Ioways sold their allotments to nontribal members. In 2004 the tribe owned around 2,707 acres, a portion of which they planted in row crops, some of which they utilized for grazing, and some which they held in the Conservation Reserve Program. The Bureau of Indian Affairs holds a portion of the land on the reservation in trust, while individual tribal members own other land individually.[6]

The reservation of the Ioway Tribe of Kansas and Nebraska today shows that the Ioways are living a markedly different existence from before the Civil War. After driving out of the Missouri River valley and away from the small town of White Cloud, Kansas, and traveling west for a few miles along country roads, visitors are greeted by a large sign on which the words "White Cloud Casino" are surrounded by an eagle feather motif rendered in brightly painted sheet metal and plastic. Large black silhouettes representing the original clan ancestors adorn the casino's exterior walls: Earth clans on one side of the main entrance and Sky clans on the other side. Inside the casino visitors will find walls covered with pictures representing the Ioways' past. A bear claw necklace, which is believed to have been worn by Francis White Cloud's son James White Cloud, is beautifully displayed in a new exhibit case. The casino is part of the Iowa tribal complex, a collection of modern buildings that includes a convenience store, a restaurant, a rodeo arena, tourist cabins, tribal government offices, wind turbines, and a day-care center. Tucked into a valley just northwest of the office near Roy's Creek, travelers will discover an arbor, floodlights, and a concrete restroom building that mark the spot where the annual fall powwow and encampment takes place on the third weekend of each September.

Ten miles to the south, near the town of Highland, Kansas, a portion of Samuel Irvin and William Hamilton's Presbyterian mission school still stands, hidden from the main road by a large grain-processing facility and a grove of trees. The Kansas State Historical Society owns the historic building and, until a few years ago, operated it as the Native American Heritage Museum. Inside, rooms that once featured displays about Reverend Irvin and the history of the mission school on the ground floor and traditional arts and crafts—drums, powwow regalia, wooden flutes, and beadwork—on the second floor, now stand empty.

These few sites notwithstanding, there is very little visible evidence to indicate to visitors traveling through Doniphan County, Kansas, and Richardson County, Nebraska, that they are in Indian country. In the recent past much of the Iowa Tribe's income has been derived from cattle feedlots, fields of row crops, a truck stop, and an ethanol-processing plant, and of course, the casino. Drivers passing through the area are far more likely to notice agricultural machinery dotting the landscape than they are to catch a glimpse of the low bent-willow frame of a sweat lodge, the mounded shape of a traditional bark-covered *chakadutha* lodge, or even the conical form of a teepee.

This brings to mind George Catlin's observation that by 1832 the Ioways were "the farthest departed from primitive modes" of all the tribes in the region and were "depending chiefly on their cornfields for their subsistence."[7] Even before their move to the Great Nemaha Agency Catlin observed that the U.S. government's process of forced assimilation was already having an effect on the Ioways. That process started during the first two decades they spent on the reservation. Despite their protests and resistance the Ioways, like all Native people in North America, were pushed to leave behind the traditional ways that had served them since time immemorial and to become more like the white settlers who surrounded their land.

The Ioways have survived by balancing the tensions between the pull of the past and the lure of the future. In the process they have adapted and learned not only to survive but to succeed in the modern world. The Ioway language, the traditional clan system, traditional Ioway ceremonies, and other forms of Indigenous knowledge are all in danger of being lost as a direct result of the work that was carried out over 150 years ago on the Great Nemaha Agency.

There is, however, a resurgence of some elements of Ioway tradition as members of the community realize the importance of what is being lost. Both branches of the Ioway Tribe are working to revive their language and other traditions. The Iowa Tribe of Oklahoma opened the Bah Khoje Xla Chi (Grey Snow Eagle House) in 2006. This rehabilitation aviary has, as of March 2013, released eight bald eagles and housed forty-six eagles that were not releasable. The staff and volunteers of the facility maintain permits from the U.S. Fish and Wildlife Service that allow them to utilize their population of eagles for education and scientific studies. The Ioways are also permitted to distribute naturally molted eagle feathers from the aviary to tribal members for ceremonial purposes.[8]

The Iowa Tribe of Kansas and Nebraska has recently added a Tribal Historic Preservation Office (THPO) to their tribal government. This office is responsible for protecting historical resources on the reservation. It also consults with museums that have Ioway artifacts in their collections and works with government agencies to ensure that Ioway-related burial sites are treated in accordance with mandates set out in the Native American Graves Protection and Repatriation Act (NAGPRA). The office is also undertaking an initiative that would bring historical displays and museum exhibits to the reservation. The Báxoje Wósgaci (Ioway Tribal Museum and Cultural Heritage Center) is envisioned as a home for stories about the Ioways' past and a place where tribal members can explore the issue of what it means to be Ioway in a world that continues to change and evolve.

Notes

INTRODUCTION

1. In this book, the Great Nemaha Subagency is sometimes referred to as the Great Nemaha Agency. Between 1837 and 1851, it operated as a subagency under the Upper Missouri Agency in present-day Bellevue, Nebraska. On July 1, 1851, a reorganization of the Bureau of Indian Affairs elevated the facility to full agency status. Records for both the subagency and the agency are included in National Archives Record Group 75, Letters Received by the Office of Indian Affairs, 1824–1881, Great Nemaha Agency, 1837–1876, Microcopy 234 (referred to hereafter as GNA).

2. Francis Paul Prucha, *The Indians in American Society: From the Revolutionary War to the Present* (Berkeley: University of California Press, 1885), 7.

3. Ibid., 8.

4. Ibid., 9.

5. Ibid., 11.

6. Martha Royce Blaine, *The Ioway Indians* (1979; Norman: University of Oklahoma Press, 1995), 205–68.

7. Joseph B. Herring, *The Enduring Indians of Kansas: A Century and a Half of Acculturation* (Lawrence: University Press of Kansas, 1990), 70–97.

8. Michael C. Coleman, *Presbyterian Missionary Attitudes toward American Indians, 1837–1893* (Jackson: University Press of Mississippi, 1985), 5–6.

9. Willard Rollings, *Unaffected by the Gospel: Osage Resistance to the Christian Invasion, 1673–1906: A Cultural Victory* (Albuquerque: University of New Mexico Press, 2004).

10. See Blaine, *Ioway Indians*; Greg Olson, *The Ioway in Missouri* (Columbia: University of Missouri Press, 2008).

1. THE LONG ROAD TO THE GREAT NEMAHA AGENCY

1. James L. Theler and Robert F. Boszhardt, *Twelve Millennia: Archaeology of the Upper Mississippi River Valley* (Iowa City: University of Iowa Press, 2003), 33–37, 157–66; Lynn M. Alex, *Iowa's Archaeological Past* (Iowa City: University of Iowa Press, 2000), 185–88; Duane C. Anderson, "Iowa Ethnology: A Review, Part 1," *Annals of Iowa* 41 (1971–73): 1230–31; Brian Fagan, *The Little Ice Age: How Climate Made History* (New York: Basic Books, 2000), 3–79; Orr and Keyes from Alex, *Iowa's Archaeological Past*, 186.

2. Lance M. Foster, "The Ioway and the Landscape of Southeast Iowa," *Ioway Cultural Institute*, http://ioway.nativeweb.org/iowaylibrary/seiowa.htm, 5; Alfred W. Crosby, *Ecological Imperialism: The Biological Expansion of Europe* (Cambridge: Cambridge University Press, 1986), 195–216; Alfred W. Crosby, *The Columbian Exchange: Biological and Cultural Consequences of 1492* (Westport, Conn.: Greenwood Publishing: 1972), 35–63; Timothy E. Roberts and Christy S. Richers, "Historical Iowa Settlements in the Grand River Basin of Missouri and Iowa," *Missouri Archaeologist* 57 (December 1996): 1–36; Jimm GoodTracks, "The Name 'Ioway'," electronic mail post to the Siouan Language listserv, March 8, 2012, at http://listserv.linguistlist.org/pipermail/siouan/2012-March/008616.html.

3. Blaine, *Ioway Indians*, 17; Zachary Gussow, *An Anthropological Report: Sac, Fox and Iowa Indians* (New York: Garland Press, 1974), 1:35.

4. Gussow, *Sac, Fox and Iowa*, 35–36.

5. Mildred Mott Wedel, "Peering at the Ioway Indians through the Mist of Time, 1650–c. 1700," *Journal of the Iowa Archeological Society* 33 (1986): 46–47; Gussow, *Sac, Fox and Iowa*, 36–37; Tanis C. Thorne, *The Many Hands of My Relations: French and Indians on the Lower Missouri* (Columbia: University of Missouri Press, 1996), 57.

6. De La Salle's proclamation of ownership over land that was already occupied by Indigenous people was legitimized by the legal concept known as the Discovery Doctrine. The doctrine dates back to 1452, when Pope Nicholas V decreed that European nations had the right to claim land occupied by populations who were not the subjects of a European Christian monarch, because these populations were seen as enemies of the Roman Catholic Church. First used during the Crusades, the doctrine was used extensively as European nations explored North America and became a part of U.S. Law in 1823 with the Supreme Court's ruling in *Johnson v. McIntosh*. In that decision, Chief Justice John Marshall wrote that upon discovery, Indigenous nations lost "their rights to complete sovereignty, as independent nations" and retained only the right to occupy land in the United States. See Steve Newcomb, "Five Hundred Years of Injustice: The Legacy of

Fifteenth Century Injustice," *Indigenous Law Institute*, at http://ili.nativeweb.org /sdrm_art.html.

7. Anderson, "Ioway Ethnology," 1236.

8. Blaine, *Ioway Indians*, 48–49; Gussow, *Sac, Fox and Iowa*, 40; Saul Schwartz, "Iowaville in Perspectives: Expansive Ethnohistory at an Ioway Indian Village" (honors thesis, Beloit College, 2008), 16.

9. Blaine, *Ioway Indians*, 83: Thorne, *Many Hands of My Relations*, 110–12.

10. Gussow, *Sac, Fox and Iowa*, 44; Saul Schwartz, "Iowaville Historic Context," in Cindy Peterson, ed., *Archaeological Study of Iowaville, a 1765–1824 Ioway (Báxoje) Village in Van Buren County, Iowa* (Iowa City: Office of the State Archaeologist, 2012), 4.

11. Gussow, *Sac, Fox and Iowa*, 42–44; Schwartz, "Iowaville Historic Context," 4. Also see John Melish's map of the United States in Olson, *The Ioway in Missouri*, 47.

12. Lance M. Foster, "Treaties," *Ioway Cultural Institute*, http://ioway.nativeweb .org/history/treaties.htm; Blaine, *Ioway Indians*, 81–82.

13. Blaine, *Ioway Indians*, 82; Gussow, *Sac, Fox and Iowa*, 49.

14. Louise Barry, *The Beginning of the West: Annals of the Kansas Gateway to the American West, 1540–1854* (Topeka: Kansas State Historical Society, 1972), 52; Blaine, *Ioway Indians*, 90–92.

15. An earlier smallpox epidemic that struck the Ioways in the mid-1870s had killed nearly one half of the tribe. See Schwartz, "Iowaville Historic Context," 5.

16. Michael Dickey, "The Ioway Indians: Britain's Ally in the West?" 1st U.S. Infantry and Missouri Rangers, accessed January 22, 2004, http://usregular0 .tripod.com/ioway/about page 6; John Bradbury, "Bradbury's Travels," in *Early Western Travels, 1748–1846*, ed. Reuben Gold Thwaites (Cleveland: Arthur H. Clark, 1905), 5:52.

17. Blaine, *Ioway Indians*, 96.

18. Ibid., 114–15; Foster, "Landscape of Southeast Iowa," about page 6; Dickey, "The Ioway Indians," about pages 9–10.

19. "Treaty with the Iowa, 1815," in Charles J. Kappler, ed., *Indian Affairs: Laws and Treaties* (Washington, DC: Government Printing Office, 1904), 2:122–23; Blaine, *Ioway Indians*, 115–16.

20. Blaine, *Ioway Indians*, 109; Gussow, *Sac, Fox and Iowa*, 43.

21. Accounts of the attack on Iowaville place the date variously between 1819 and 1823. Blaine, *Ioway Indians*, 130; A. R. Fulton, *Red Men of Iowa* (Des Moines: Mills & Company, 1882), 120; Foster, "Landscape of Southeast Iowa," about pages 1–5; Frank E. Stevens, *The Black Hawk War* (Chicago: Frank E. Stevens, 1903), 68–70; Benjamin O'Fallon to John C. Calhoun, September 25, 1819, in *Territorial Papers*, ed. Clarence Edwin Carter (Washington, DC: Government Printing Office, 1949), 15:562–63; Schwartz, "Iowaville Historic Context," 5–6.

22. Theodore W. Taylor, *The Bureau of Indian Affairs* (Boulder, Colo.: Westview Press, 1984), 10, 34; William Clark to James Barbour, March 1, 1825, in Blaine, *Ioway Indians*, 147–48.

23. Clark to Barbour, March 1, 1825, in Blaine, *Ioway Indians*, 147–48.

24. Blaine, *Ioway Indians*, 142; "Treaty with the Iowa, 1824," in Kappler, *Indian Affairs*, 2:208–209.

25. *The Heritage of Buchanan County* (St. Joseph, Mo.: Missouri River Heritage Association, 1984), 1, 56; John Dougherty to William Clark, August 20, 1827, Dougherty Letter Book, 1826–1829, Western Historical Manuscripts Collection, Columbia, Missouri.

26. "Moanahonga," in Thomas L. McKenney and James Hall, *History of the Indian Tribes of North America* (Philadelphia: D. Rice & Co., 1872), 1:177–83.

27. During the border dispute and trial, Great Walker went by the name Big Neck. See Dorothy Caldwell, "The Big Neck Affair: Tragedy and Farce on the Missouri Frontier," *Missouri Historical Review* 64 (July 1970): 391–412; Derek R. Everett, "To Shed Our Blood for Our Beloved Territory: The Iowa-Missouri Borderland," *Annals of Iowa* 67 (Fall 2008): 269–97.

28. "Treaty with the Sioux, etc., 1825," in Kappler, *Indian Affairs*, 2:250–55.

29. "Treaty with the Sauk and Foxes, etc., 1830," in Kappler, *Indian Affairs*, 2:305–10. Raining is often referred to in contemporary documents as Walking Rain. However, linguist Jimm Goodtracks suggests that Raining is a more accurate translation of his Ioway name. Ñi'yuMa'ñi (GoodTracks), email to the author, August 20, 2005.

30. "Extracts from Minutes of a Council held at Prairie du Chien, Wednesday, July 7, 1830," Documents Relating to the Negotiation of Ratified and Unratified Treaties with Various Indian Tribes, 1801–69 (National Archives Microcopy T494, roll 2), 17.

31. Thorne, *Many Hands of My Relations*, 141–45.

32. Blaine, *Ioway Indians*, 249; Thorne, *Many Hands of My Relations*, 141–43, 214–20.

33. Thomas H. Benton to John Eaton, December 21, 1829 (Iowa Agency Records, M234, roll 362).

34. Andrew Hughes to P. B. Porter, December 22, 1828 (Iowa Agency Records, M234, roll 362).

35. "Treaty with the Iowa, Etc. 1836," in Kappler, *Indian Affairs*, 2:468–70.

2. "THE HOUSE IS EMPTY"

1. The epigraph is from Samuel Irvin, in Presbyterian Board of Foreign Missionaries (hereafter BFM), *Fourth Annual Report of the Board of Foreign Missionaries of the Presbyterian Church of the United States of America* (New York: BFM, 1841), 6.

2. Wedel, "Peering at the Ioway Indians," 46–47.

3. William Hamilton quoted in James Owen Dorsey, "A Study of Siouan Cults," *Eleventh Annual Report of the Bureau of Ethnology to the Secretary of the Smithsonian Institution, 1889–1890* (Washington, DC: Government Printing Office, 1894), 423–24.

4. Jimm GoodTracks, electronic correspondence with the author, June 29, 2003, and April 6, 2005.

5. Alanson Skinner, "Traditions of the Iowa Indians," *Journal of American Folklore* 38 (October–December 1925): 438; GoodTracks, e-mail correspondence with the author, September 15, 2003, and April 6, 2005.

6. Carolyn Merchant, *Ecological Revolutions: Nature, Gender, and Science in New England* (Chapel Hill: University of North Carolina Press, 1989), 44, 50.

7. Ibid., 74–81; Blaine, *Ioway Indians*, 226–27; Lance Foster, "Ancestral Ways of Life," *Ioway Cultural Institute*, http://ioway.nativeweb.org/culture/ancestrallife .htm.

8. Merchant, *Ecological Revolutions*, 205.

9. Rollings, *Unaffected by the Gospel*, 46–47.

10. Ibid.; Coleman, *Presbyterian Missionary Attitudes*, 9–11.

11. G. J. Garraghan, *The Jesuits of the Middle United States* (Chicago: Loyola University Press, 1983), 1:147–69.

12. Coleman, *Presbyterian Missionary Attitudes*, 11–13.

13. Ibid.; William Hamilton, "The Iowa and Sac Mission," c. fall 1850 (American Indian Correspondence, Presbyterian Historical Society Collection of Missionaries' Letters, 1833–93 [hereafter PHS], box 3).

14. BFM, *First Annual Report* (1838), 14–15; Jennie Chin, Joy Harnett, and Suzette McCord-Rogers, *Native American Heritage Museum at the Highland Mission State Historic Site* (Topeka: Kansas State Historical Society, 1996), 5; Coleman, *Presbyterian Missionary Attitudes*, 4.

15. Coleman, *Presbyterian Missionary Attitudes*, 15–17.

16. Ibid., 5–6, 80, 140, 155–59.

17. Ibid., 4, 23, 25.

18. William Hamilton to Walter Lowrie, September 29, 1852 (American Indian Correspondence, PHS, box 3).

19. Joseph B. Herring, "Presbyterian Ethnologists among the Iowa and Sac Indians, 1837–1853," *American Presbyterians* 65 (Fall 1987): 196–97; Pryor Plank, "The Ioway, Sac and Fox Indian Mission and Its Missionaries, Rev. Samuel Irvin and Wife," in *Transactions of the Kansas State Historical Society, 1907–1908* (Topeka: Kansas State Historical Society, 1908), 10:319.

20. "Walter Lowrie, Secretary of the Senate, 1825–1836," *Art and History, U.S. Senate*, http://www.senate.gov/artandhistory/history/common/generic/SOS_Walter _Lowrie.htm; Coleman, *Presbyterian Missionary Attitudes*, 17.

21. The missionaries wrote an ethnographic article about the Ioways and the Sacs. See Samuel Irvin and William Hamilton, "Iowa and Sac Tribes," in Henry R.

Schoolcraft, *Information Respecting the History, Conditions and Prospects of the Indian Tribes of the United States*, vol. 3 (Philadelphia: Lippincott, Grambo & Co., 1853).

22. Coleman, *Presbyterian Missionary Attitudes*, 80–81.

23. BFM, *First Annual Report*, 14–15; Hamilton, "Iowa and Sac Mission," 1–2; Barry, *Beginning of the West*, 337.

24. Samuel M. Irvin, entry for January 14, 1842, Diaries of Samuel M. Irvin (Kansas Historical Society, Microfilm MS 89); Congrave Jackson to Joshua Pilcher, January 31, 1841 (GNA, M234, roll 307).

25. Hamilton, "Iowa and Sac Mission," 3–4.

26. William P. Richardson, "Map showing the principal improvements within the Great Nemahaw sub agency," 1843 (GNA, M234, roll 307).

27. Irvin to Walter Lowrie, July 10, 1851 (American Indian Correspondence, PHS, box 3).

28. "Mission to the Iowa and Sac Indians," in BFM, *Fourth Annual Report* (1841), 5–6; For more on Jeffrey Deroine, see Greg Olson, "Slave, Trader, Interpreter, and World Traveler: The Remarkable Life of Jeffrey Deroine," *Missouri Historical Review* 107 (July 2013): 222–30; Hamilton, "Iowa and Sac Mission," 2.

29. William Richardson to David D. Mitchell, November 1, 1841 (GNA, M234, roll 307); Barry, *Beginning of the West*, 441, 533.

30. Lela Barnes, "Notes on Imprints from Highland: The Second Point of Printing in Kansas," *Kansas Historical Quarterly* 8 (May 1939): 140; "The Mission of the Iowa and Sac Indians," in BFM, *Sixth Annual Report* (1843), 6–7; Blaine, *Ioway Indians*, 173; "The Mission of the Iowa and Sac Indians," in BFM, *Seventh Annual Report* (1844), 10.

31. "The Mission of the Iowa and Sac Indians," in BFM, *Eighth Annual Report* (1845), 7–8.

32. Hamilton, "Iowa and Sac Mission," 9–10; Alfred Vaughn to David Mitchell, September 19 [?], 1849, and James Carlton to E. V. Sumner, September 1849 (GNA, M234, roll 308, frames 140–41, 152–56).

33. "Mission among the Iowa and Sac Indians," in BFM, *Fifth Annual Report* (1842), 8.

34. Hamilton, "Iowa and Sac Mission," 10.

35. Lance M. Foster, *Sacred Bundles of the Ioway Indians* (Master's thesis, Iowa State University, 1994), 38–40; Herring, *Enduring Indians*, 77–78; Dorsey, "Study of Siouan Cults," 425–27; Skinner, "Traditions of the Iowa Indians," 427–41.

36. Bayard Taylor, *Views Afoot: Or, Europe Seen with Knapsack and Staff* (1846; reprint, The Literature Network, Internet, http://www.online-literature.com/bayard-taylor/views-a-foot/1), about page 3.

37. The name WašíMáñi (Always Dancing) is based on the English name he was sometimes called, Fast Dancer. Martha Royce Blaine referred to him as Washkamonya (Fast Dancer). Based on this, linguist Jimm GoodTracks has also provided the possible alternate names Wá^n^šhink^Máñi (Man Walks or Travels) and

WašíˆWáñe (Dance Man or Person). Jimm GoodTracks, e-mail to the author, July 6, 2014; Blaine, *Ioway Indians*, 231.

38. In Blaine, the name appears as *Wa-ta-we-bu-ka-na* (the Commanding General). From this GoodTracks has proposed that the Ioway name may have been Wéxawìrugra[n], which can be literally translated to mean "Excelled He Rules," GoodTracks, e-mail to the author, July 6, 2014; Blaine, *Ioway Indians*, 231.

39. George Catlin, *Adventures of the Ojibbeway and Ioway Indians in England, France, and Belgium* (1852; reprint, Whitefish, Mont.: Kessinger Publishing, n.d.): 2:54–56.

40. Blaine, *The Ioway Indians*, 233.

41. Ibid., 225.

42. Catlin, *Adventures of the Ojibbeway and Ioway*, 93–94; The Ioway name ThíNádaye is based on the English name Blistered Feet, which appears in Blaine, *Ioway Indians*, 229–31. Jimm GoodTracks, email to the author, July 6, 2014.

43. Catlin, *Adventures of the Ojibbeway and Ioway*, 152.

44. Ibid., 99–101.

45. Ibid., 220–21.

46. Rollings, *Unaffected by the Gospel*, 88, 95, 110–13.

47. BFM, *First Annual Report*, 14–15; BFM, *Second Annual Report* (1839), 15.

48. Hamilton, "Iowa and Sac Mission," 10–11.

3. "USEFUL IN THIS WORLD AND HAPPY IN THE NEXT"

1. Michael Katz quoted in Michael C. Coleman, *American Indian Children at School, 1850–1930* (Jackson: University of Mississippi Press, 1993), 38; James B. Ramsey quoted in Coleman, *Presbyterian Missionary Attitudes*, 16.

2. "Notchimine," in McKenney and Hall, *Indian Tribes*, 2:181–82.

3. Jimm G. Goodtracks, "Oral Literature Tradition" (unpublished manuscript, collection of the author), 3–6; Alanson Skinner, "Ethnology of the Ioway and Sauk Indians," *Bulletin of the Public Museum of the City of Milwaukee* 5 (1923–26): 253.

4. Skinner, "Traditions of the Iowa Indians," 487–88.

5. Goodtracks, "Oral Literature Tradition," 4.

6. Skinner, "Traditions of the Iowa Indians," 503–506.

7. Garraghan, *Jesuits*, 1:150–53, 168.

8. Ibid., 162–63; E. Laveille, SJ, *The Life of Father DeSmet, SJ* (New York: P. J. Kennedy and Sons, 1915), 53.

9. Garraghan, *Jesuits*, 1:162.

10. Blaine, *Ioway Indians*, 205, 226; Rudolph Friedrich Kurz, *The Journal of Rudolph Friedrich Kurz: The Life and Work of This Swiss Artist, 1846–1852* (1937; reprint, Fairfield, Wash.: Ye Galleon Press, 1969), 45; Carolyn Thomas Foreman, "The Choctaw Academy," *Chronicles of Oklahoma* 6 (December 1928): 453.

11. Jacqueline Fear-Segal, *White Man's Club: Schools Race, and the Struggle of Indian Acculturation* (Lincoln: University of Nebraska Press, 2007), 21–33; Coleman, *American Indian Children*, 38–39; Sally McBeth, *Ethnic Identity and the Boarding School Experience of West Central Oklahoma American Indians* (Washington, DC: University Press of America, 1983), 75; David Wallace Adams, *Education for Extinction: American Indians and the Boarding School Experience, 1875–1928* (Lawrence: University Press of Kansas, 1995), 6.

12. Morris W. Werner, "Indian Missions in Kansas," *Kansas Heritage*, accessed March 12, 2014, http://www.kansasheritage.org/werner/mission.html; Barry, *Beginning of the West*, 179, 204–205, 275, 399.

13. Barry, *Beginning of the West*, 258–59; BFM, *Third Annual Report* (1840), 9–10: Coleman, *Presbyterian Missionary Attitudes*, 4.

14. BFM, *Second Annual Report*, 15, and *Third Annual Report*, 5–6.

15. Irvin Diary, April 29, 1841, 38; Congrave Jackson to Pilcher, January 31, 1841 (GNA, M234, roll 307); Richardson, Map of the Great Nemaha Subagency, 1843 (GNA, M234, roll 307, frame 0618).

16. Herring, *Enduring Indians*, 76–80; Hamilton, "Iowa and Sac Mission," 2–3; Barry, *Beginning of the West*, 465, 502, 533, 661.

17. Irvin Diary, April 22, 1941: 35.

18. Irvin Diary, April 23, 1841: 35.

19. BFM, *Fifth Annual Report*, 7–8.

20. No Heart and Raining may have been speaking here of the Kickapoo Academy near Fort Leavenworth. Both Catholics and Methodists operated missions there in 1842. William Richardson, "Minutes of the Ioway Nation in Council Assembled," September 7, 1842 (GNA, M234, roll 307).

21. BFM, *Seventh Annual Report*, 10.

22. William Richardson, "Annual Report of the Great Nemaha Agency," September 16, 1842 (GNA, M234, roll 307).

23. General Assembly of the Presbyterian Church of the United States of America (PCUSA), quoted in Coleman, *Presbyterian Missionary Attitudes*, 16.

24. BFM, *Seventh Annual Report*, 10.

25. BFM, *Eighth Annual Report*, 7–8; Barry, *Beginning of the West*, 528; Plank, "The Ioway, Sac and Fox Indian Mission," 315.

26. Hamilton, "Iowa and Sac Mission," 5–6.

27. BFM, *Ninth Annual Report* (1846), 5.

28. BFM, *Tenth Annual Report* (1847), 9–10, and *Eleventh Annual Report* (1848), 11–12.

29. John W. Kelly to the Commissioner of Indian Affairs [?], April 29, 1847 (GNA, M234, roll 307), 1–2.

30. Ibid., 3.

31. BFM, *Ninth Annual Report*, 5.

32. Hamilton to Lowrie, September 30, 1850, Irvin to Lowrie, January 29, 1852 (American Indian Correspondence, PHS, box 3).

33. Hamilton and Irvin to Lowrie, November 22, 1851 [?] (American Indian Correspondence, PHS, box 3).

34. "Report for the Quarter Ending December 31, 1851: Iowa and Sac Mission," and Irvin to Lowrie, November 13, 1854 (American Indian Correspondence, PHS, box 3).

35. Coleman, *Presbyterian Missionary Attitudes*, 17; Irvin to Lowrie, August 18, 1853 (American Indian Correspondence, PHS, box 3).

36. Irvin to Lowrie, August 18, 1853 (American Indian Correspondence, PHS, box 3).

37. "Report of the Girl's School and the Ioways, Fall 1852, Iowa and Sac Mission," and Irvin to Richardson [?], August 31, 1852 (American Indian Correspondence, PHS, box 3); Jane Bloohm to George Catlin, May 28, 1847, in Catlin, *Adventures of the Ojibbeway and Ioway*, 330.

38. Quarterly reports for the Ioway and Sac Mission, March 31, June 30, 1851, October 31, 1852, and Irvin to Lowrie, January 29, 1852 (American Indian Correspondence, PHS, box 3).

39. Hamilton to Lowrie, October 31, 1852, ibid.

40. Abstract, *Oscar Banks et al. v. Catherine Galbraith et al.*, October term 1898 (file ID #8471, Supreme Court of Missouri files, Missouri State Archives), 65, 68.

41. BFM, *Seventh Annual Report*, 10.

42. Quarterly report of the Ioway and Sac Mission, December 31, 1851; Irvin to Lowrie, January 29, 1852; Hamilton to Lowrie, October 31, 1852 (all in American Indian Correspondence, PHS, box 3).

43. Daniel Vanderslice to Alfred Cumming, June 30, 1856 (GNA, M234, roll 308, frames 814–15); Samuel Irvin, "The School," written report to the BFM, c. 1854 (American Indian Correspondence, PHS, box 3); Vanderslice to A. M. Robinson, February 18, 1860 (GNA, M234, roll 310, frame 404).

44. BFM, *Seventh Annual Report*, 10; Irvin to Richardson [?], August 31, 1852 (American Indian Correspondence, PHS, box 3); "Board of Foreign Missions, Abstract of the Ninth Annual Report," *Minutes of the General Assembly of the Presbyterian Church of the United States of America* (Philadelphia: Clerk of the General Assembly, 1845–47), 11:361.

45. Irvin to Lowrie, August 7, 1952, and February 16, July 15, 1853 (American Indian Correspondence, PHS, box 3).

46. Ibid., March 29, 1854.

47. Irvin to Lowrie, April 27, 1859 (American Indian Correspondence, PHS, box 3); also Vanderslice to Alfred Cumming, December 26, 1854 (GNA, R234, reel 308, frames 529–31).

48. Irvin to Lowrie, January 24, 1859 (American Indian Correspondence, PHS, box 3).

49. Ibid., September 22, 1859.

50. Ibid., April 15, 1860.

51. Linda Clemmons, "'We Find It a Difficult Work': Educating Dakota Children in Missionary Homes, 1835–1862," *American Indian Quarterly* 24 (Fall 2000): 572, 578.

52. No Heart quoted in Herring, *Enduring Indians*, 76; BFM, *Seventh Annual Report*, 10.

53. Adams, *Education for Extinction*, 257.

54. Barry, *Beginning of the West*, 326, 545; Herring, *Enduring Indians*, 83.

4. A CHANGE IN IOWAY LEADERSHIP

1. Ioway-Otoe-Missouri (IOM) clan origin stories are found under the entry for the word "clan" in Jimm GoodTracks, "IOM Dictionary," in *Ioway, Otoe-Missouria Language*, http://iowayotoelang.nativeweb.org/pdf/c_engtobax2008aug 18.pdf, 3–4.

2. Lance M. Foster, "Tanji na Che: Recovering the Landscape of the Ioway," in *Ioway Cultural Institute*, http://ioway.nativeweb.org/iowaylibrary/tanji.htm/about page 9; Alanson Skinner, "Societies of the Iowa, Kansas and Ponca Indians," *Anthropological Papers of the American Museum of Natural History* 11 (1915): 729–32; GoodTracks, e-mail correspondence with the author, October 28, 2002, and March 7, 2003.

3. Blaine, *Ioway Indians*, 125; Skinner, "Societies of the Iowa, Kansas and Ponca Indians," 683–85; Skinner, "Ethnology of the Ioway and Sauk Indians," 199–200.

4. Blaine, *Ioway Indians*, 185; Skinner "Societies of the Iowa, Kansas and Ponca Indians," 686; Skinner, "Ethnology of the Ioway and Sauk Indians," 201.

5. Robert Willoughby, *The Brothers Robidoux and the Opening of the American West* (Columbia: University of Missouri Press, 2012), 34–35.

6. Blaine, *Ioway Indians*, 211–12.

7. Kurz, *The Journal*, 44; Abstract, *Banks v. Galbraith*, 22–24.

8. Kurz, *The Journal*, 50.

9. Thorne, *Many Hands of My Relations*, 135–76; Roy E. Coy and Mrs. Walter Hall, "Genealogy and History of the White Cloud Family," *Museum Graphic* 4 (Spring 1852): 8.

10. Willard H. Rollings, *The Osage: An Ethnocentric Study of Hegemony on the Prairie-Plains* (Columbia: University of Missouri Press, 1992), 157–59; Stephen Aron, *American Confluence: The Missouri Frontier from Borderland to Border State* (Bloomington: Indiana University Press, 2006), 15–16; Thorne, *Many Hands of My Relations*, 109–10.

11. In Blaine, *Ioway Indians*, the Ioway leader is identified as "Le Voleur" (The Thief). Jimm GoodTracks has translated this to the Ioway name Wamúnuge, which roughly translates as "the Thief." Jimm GoodTracks, e-mail to the author,

July 6, 2014; Blaine, *Ioway Indians*, 62–64; Dickey, "The Ioway Indians," about page 2.

12. Thorne, *Many Hands of My Relations*, 98–120; Rollings, *The Osage*, 157–59; Aron, *American Confluence*, 16–17.

13. William Clark to John Armstrong, September 12, 1813, *Territorial Papers*, 14: 697; Dickey, "The Ioway Indians," about page 6.

14. Duke Paul Wilhelm mentions Hard Heart's death in his journal entry for July 30, 1823. See Paul Wilhelm, duke of Wurttemberg, *Travels in North America, 1822–1824*, trans. W. Robert Nitske, ed. Savoie Lottinville (Norman: University of Oklahoma Press, 1973), 315–16.

15. For more on White Cloud, see Greg Olson, "Navigating the White Road: White Cloud's Struggle to Lead the Ioway along the Path of Acculturation," *Missouri Historical Review* 99 (January 2005): 93–114.

16. "Extracts from Minutes of a Council held at Prairie du Chien, Wednesday, July 7, 1830," Treaty 159 (Treaty Files, National Archives Records Administration, Microfilm Publication T494, roll 2, RG 75), 17.

17. Blaine, *Ioway Indians*, 201; "Mahaskah," in McKenney and Hall, *Indian Tribes*, 2:216–17.

18. Greg Olson, "Two Portraits, Two Legacies: Anglo-American Artists View Chief White Cloud," *Gateway* 25 (summer 2005): 21–31.

19. "Notchimine," in McKenney and Hall, *Indian Tribes*, 2:181–84.

20. "Mahaskah," in ibid., 223–24; Report to Elbert Herring, Commissioner of Indian Affairs, October 3, 1834 (GNA, M234, roll 362).

21. "Mahaskah," in McKenney and Hall, *Indian Tribes*, 2:223–24.

22. John Dougherty to John Bliss, February 14, 1829 (John Dougherty Letter Book, State Historical Society of Missouri, Columbia).

23. Dougherty to William Clark, August 28, 1835 (GNA, M234, roll 362); Blaine, *Ioway Indians*, 163.

24. For more on the legend, its history, and its continuing popularity, see Greg Olson, *Voodoo Priests, Noble Savages, and Ozark Gypsies: The Life of Folklorist Mary Alicia Owen* (Columbia: University of Missouri Press, 2012): 136–40.

25. Blaine, *Ioway Indians*, 164–69.

26. Barry, *Beginning of the West*, 735–36.

27. Ibid., 326: "Treaty with the Iowa. Etc., 1837," in Kappler, *Indian Affairs*, 2:469.

28. Dougherty to Clark, March 24, April 1838 (GNA, M234, roll 307).

29. Blaine, *Ioway Indians*, 198; William Clark to Commissioner of Indian Affairs C. A. Harris, April 2, 1838 (GNA, M234, roll 307).

30. Jonathan Bean to Pilcher, December 1, 1839 (GNA, M234, roll 307).

31. Bean to Pilcher, August 18, October 24, 1839, ibid.

32. Bean to Pilcher, December 1, 1839, ibid.; "An article of agreement made and agreed to this 23rd day of September in the year of one thousand eight

hundred and forty, between Samuel M. Irvin of the one part and the chiefs of the Ioway nation on the other part, both of the Indian Territory," September 23, 1840, ibid.

33. "Minutes of a council between the Ioway nation and sub agent William Richardson," 7 September 1842 (ibid.), 4; Kéramañi's name appears in the treaty minutes as Caromonga. Kéra is a traditional bear clan name meaning clear sky. Jimm GoodTracks suggests the name Kéramañi means Clearing Sky. GoodTracks, electronic mail to the author, July 1, 2015.

34. Dougherty to Clark, August 28, 1835 (Ioway Agency Records, M234, roll 362, about frame 490).

35. BFM, *Fourth Annual Report*, 5–6, and *Fifth Annual Report*, 7–8.

36. "Ioway Nation in Council Assembled," September 7, 1842 (GNA, M234, roll 307).

37. "Great Time Among the Indians—Heap Dog!" *White Cloud Kansas Chief*, March 25, 1858, 2.

38. Richardson to Mitchell, November 1, 1841 (GNA, M234, roll 307).

39. "Minutes of a council between the Ioway nation and sub agent William Richardson," September 7, 1842 (GNA, M234, roll 307).

40. "A talk or council held with the chiefs and braves of the Iowa tribe of Indians by T. H. Harvey in the chapel at the mission in the Great Nemaha sub agency on the 14th April, 1846," (GNA, M234, roll 307).

41. Blaine, *Ioway Indians*, 237–40.

42. Subagent Alfred Vaughn to Thomas H. Harvey, June 1, 1848 (GNA, M234, roll 307).

43. James Henry Carlton to E. V. Sumner, September 1849 (GNA, M234, roll 308, frames 152–56); Alfred Vaughn to David D. Mitchell (Superintendent of Indian Affairs in St. Louis), September 19, 1849 (GNA, M234, roll 308, frames 140–41); Blaine, *Ioway Indians*, 242–43.

44. "Something About White Cloud," *White Cloud Kansas Chief*, November 12, 1857, 2.

45. Ibid.; "The Indians," *White Cloud Kansas Chief*, October 1, 1857; *White Cloud Kansas Chief*, June 24, 1858, 2.

46. Blaine refers to Ragráshe as Naggarash, Laggarash, or British. Jimm Good-Tracks has provided "Ragráshe" as the Ioway word meaning "British." It is not likely that the Ioway leader Wamúnuge (He Who Steals) mentioned here is the same Wamúnuge (The Thief) who met with the British in 1776. Jimm Good-Tracks, e-mail to the author, July 6, 2014; Irvin to Lowrie, April 20, 1854 (American Indian Correspondence, PHS, box 3).

47. Barry, *Beginning of the West*, 1091; Richardson to Mitchell, May 3, 1851 (GNA, M234, reel 308).

48. Kurz, *The Journal*, 40.

49. "Our Red Brethren," *White Cloud Kansas Chief*, July 9, 1857, 2.

50. "Another Indian Killed," *White Cloud Kansas Chief*, December 23, 1858, 2; "An Indian Murdered," *White Cloud Kansas Chief*, December 30, 1858, 3; "Indirectly Committing Murder," *White Cloud Kansas Chief*, December 6, 1860, 2.

51. Blaine, *Ioway Indians*, 259–60; "Indian 'Shin-Dig,'" *White Cloud Kansas Chief*, August 11, 1859, 2.

52. Clark to Barbour, 1 March 1825, quoted in Blaine, *Ioway Indians*, 147–48.

5. CROOKED FATHERS AND NEGLECTED CHILDREN

1. Between 1824 and 1847, the federal agency responsible for Native people was called the Office of Indian Affairs. In 1847 the agency was renamed the Bureau of Indian Affairs. In 1849 the bureau was transferred from the Department of War to the Department of the Interior.

2. Brigadier General Henry Atkinson to Isaac McCoy, July 31, 1837, in Barry, *Beginning of the West*, 329; J. W. Denver to W. M. Stark, March 12, 1858 (GNA, M234, reel 309, frames 0837–38).

3. Subagent Hughes to Commissioner of Indian Affairs Carey A. Harris, January 12, 1838 (GNA, M234, reel 307).

4. Congressman John Miller to James M. Hughes, January 17, 1838 (GNA, M234, roll 307); Blaine, *Ioway Indians*, 164–67.

5. Andrew S. Hughes to Carey A. Harris, January 12, 1838, and James M. Hughes to T. Hartley Crawford, February 20, 1845 (GNA, M234 roll 307); Barry, *Beginning of the West*, 355, 362, 364, 388, 422. On the relationship between Dougherty and Pilcher see Mark William Kelly, *Lost Voices on the Missouri: John Dougherty and the Indian Frontier* (Leavenworth: Sam Clark Publishing, 2013), 572–75; Ernest L. Schusky, "The Upper Missouri Indian Agency, 1819–1868," *Missouri Historical Review* 65 (April 1971): 255, 258.

6. Kelly, *Lost Voices*, 580–81.

7. Barry, *Beginning of the West*, 388, 422; Pilcher to Commissioner of Indian Affairs T. Hartley Crawford, April 30, 1839 (GNA, M234, roll 307).

8. Pilcher to Bean, August 18, 1839, Bean to Pilcher, October 24, December 1, 1839 (GNA, M234, roll 307).

9. Bean to Pilcher, October 24, December 1, 1839, ibid.

10. Irvin was later hired to serve as the official interpreter for the Ioways from January 1842 until September 1844. "Article of agreement made and agreed to this 23rd day of September in the year of one thousand eight hundred and forty, between Samuel M. Irvin of the one part and the chiefs of the Ioway nation on the other part, both of the Indian Territory" (GNA, M234, roll 307); Barry, *Beginning of the West*, 387, 502, 533.

11. Barry, *Beginning of the West*, 423, 441.

12. Blaine, *Ioway Indians*, 245; John McNamara quoted in Charles Clark, "W. P. Richardson," accessed February 16, 2014, http://kansasboguslegislature.org /members/richardson_w_p.html.

13. Richardson to Mitchell, November 1, 1841 (GNA, M234, roll 307).

14. Ibid.; Richardson, "On the Ioway Nation in Council Assembled," September 7, 1842 (GNA, M234, roll 307).

15. Congressman James M. Hughes to Commissioner of Indian Affairs T. Hartley Crawford, February 20, 1845 (GNA, M234, roll 307).

16. Richardson to James K. Polk, 18 July 1845 (GNA, M234, roll 307).

17. Armstrong McClintock to unknown recipient, December 25, 31, 1845 (GNA, M234, roll 307).

18. Harvey to William Medill, February 4, 1846, and James M. Hughes to Medill, April 2, 1846 (GNA, M234, roll 307).

19. "A Talk in Council held by T. H. Harvey, Superintendent of Indian Affairs, with the Ioway Indian on the 10th of April 1846 in the Chapel of the Mission in the Great Nemaha Agency," and "A Talk in Council with the Chiefs and Braves of the Ioway Tribe by T. H. Harvey in the Chapel at the Mission in the Great Nemaha Subagency on the 14th April 1846" (GNA, M234, roll 307).

20. Harvey to Medill, April 27, 1846 (GNA, M234, roll 307).

21. Bella M. Hughes to William S. Macy, October 20, 1845, and Harvey McKee to James K. Polk, October 25, 1845 (GNA, M234, roll 307).

22. George R. Gibson to unknown recipient, 18 May 1846 (GNA, M234, roll 307).

23. Hamilton and Irvin to Lowrie, April 1, 1851 (American Indian Correspondence, PHS, box 3); James M. Hughes to Medill, April 2, 1846 (GNA, M234, roll 307).

24. Samuel Hall to David Rice Atchison, January 22, 1847 (GNA, M234, roll 307).

25. Employees of the Great Nemaha Agency to Medill, January 21, 1847 (GNA, M234, roll 307).

26. John Kelly to William L. Marcy, April 29, 1847 (GNA, M234, roll 307).

27. Blaine, *Ioway Indians*, 245; Lowrie to Thomas Ewing, October 1849 (GNA, M234, roll 307); Schusky, "Upper Missouri Indian Agency," 160–61.

28. Richardson to Commissioner of Indian Affairs Orlando Brown, October 4, 1843 (GNA, M234, reel 308, frames 143–44).

29. Irvin and Hamilton to Thomas Ewing, November 28, 1849 (GNA, M234, roll 307).

30. "List of Employees at the Great Nemaha Agency, September 30, 1851" (GNA, M234, roll 307); Hamilton and Irvin to Lowrie, April 1, 1851 (American Indian Correspondence, PHS, box 3).

31. Clark, "W. P. Richardson," http://kansasboguslegislature.org.

32. Irvin to Lowrie, July 15, 1853 (American Indian Correspondence, PHS, box 3).

33. Ibid., October 5, 1853.

34. Ibid.; Barry, *Beginning of the West*, 1138.

35. "Treaty with the Iowa, 1854" and "Treaty with the Sauk and Foxes of Missouri, 1854," in Kappler, *Indian Affairs*, 2:628–33.

36. Ibid.

37. John W. Foreman to Irvin, June 24, 1854, Irvin to Lowrie, June 28, August 15, 1854 (American Indian Correspondence, PHS, box 3).

38. Irvin to Lowrie, February 8, 1855, February 12, 1857, August 16, 1868 (American Indian Correspondence, PHS, box 3).

39. Blaine, *Ioway Indians*, 250.

40. Vanderslice to George Manypenny, February 6, 1857 (GNA, M234, roll 307, frames 587–88).

41. Lewis Henry Morgan quoted in Blaine, *Ioway Indians*, 250–51.

6. EXPANDING HORIZONS AND CONSTRICTING BOUNDARIES

1. George Catlin, *Letters and Notes on the North American Indians* (1842; reprint, North Dighton, Mass.: JG Press, 1995), 2:25; Joseph B. Herring, "Selling the 'Noble Savage' Myth: George Catlin and the Iowa Indians in Europe, 1843–1845," *Kansas History: A Journal of the Central Plains* 29 (winter 2006–2007): 231.

2. Catlin, *Letters and Notes*, 2:26.

3. Herring, "Selling the 'Noble Savage' Myth," 231.

4. Taylor, *Views Afoot*, 3.

5. The names in this list have been translated into the Ioway language by Jimm GoodTracks and Sky Campbell from the phonetic spellings and English translations that are listed in Blaine's, *Ioway Indians*, 231. Rúúht^ánweMi (Strutting Pigeon Woman) or Ruton-ye-we-ma (Strutting Pigeon), Náx^ún Máñi (Hears Intermittently) or No-ho-mun-ya (One Who Gives No Attention), Jimm GoodTracks, email to the author, July 6, 2014. Blaine, *Ioway Indians*, 229–31; Herring. "Selling the 'Noble Savage' Myth," 238; Benita Eisler, *The Red Man's Bones: George Catlin, Artist and Showman* (New York: W. W. Norton, 2013), 312–15, 317.

6. Herring. "Selling the 'Noble Savage' Myth," 236–38; Eisler, *Red Man's Bones*, 312–13.

7. David Bernstein, "'We Are Not Now as We Once Were:' Iowa Indians' Political and Economic Adaptations during U.S. Incorporation," *Ethnohistory* 54, no. 4 (2007): 627; Blaine, *Ioways Indians*, 229.

8. Herring, "Selling the 'Noble Savage' Myth," 238.

9. Irvin to Catlin, May 24, 1847, from Catlin, *Adventures of the Ojibbeway and Ioway*, 2:327.

10. Catlin, *Adventures of the Ojibbeway and Ioway*, 33.

11. Ibid., 5–6; Herring. "Selling the 'Noble Savage' Myth," 237.

12. Herring, "Selling the 'Noble Savage' Myth," 240.

13. Irvin to Catlin, May 24, 1847, from Catlin, *Adventures of the Ojibbeway and Ioway*, 2:328.

14. Blaine, *Ioways Indians*, 234–35; Herring, "Selling the 'Noble Savage' Myth," 242; Bernstein, "We Are Not Now as We Once Were," 616–18; Roy W. Meyer, "The Iowa Indians, 1836–1885," *Kansas Historical Quarterly* 29 (1962): 287–88.

15. "Treaty with the Iowa, etc., 1836," in Kappler, *Indian Affairs*, 2:468.

16. Robert J. Willoughby, *Robidoux's Town: A Nineteenth-Century History of St. Joseph, Missouri* (Westphalia, Mo.: Westphalia Printing, 1997): 1, 31–38, 55–67.

17. Barry, *Beginning of the West*, 508, 848–49, 851, 862.

18. "A Travel Diary in 1854 by Sarah Sutton," in Dale Morgan, ed., *Overland in 1846: Diaries and Letters of the California-Oregon Trail* (Lincoln: University of Nebraska Press, 1993), 7:33.

19. "The Diary of Sarah Davis," in ibid., 2:174.

20. Pete Fee, unrecorded conversation with the author, St. Joseph, Missouri, March 23, 2013.

21. Mary Alicia Owen, "Poor Lucy" (typewritten manuscript, Archive of Women Writers along the Rivers, Special Collections, Missouri Western State University Library, St. Joseph, Missouri, no date). Also see Owen, "Legends of St. Joseph" (newspaper clipping dated December 3, 1916, Vertical file, Biography: Owen, Mary Alicia, St. Joseph Public Library, St. Joseph, Missouri).

22. C. W. Cooke and Vincent Geiger quoted in Jacqueline A. Lewin and Marilyn S. Taylor, *The St. Joe Road: A Traveler's Guide from the Missouri River to the Junction of the St. Joe and Independence Roads* (St. Joseph, Mo.: St. Joseph Museum, 1992), 24.

23. James Hutchens quoted in ibid., 26; Barry, *Beginning of the West*, 911, 922–23.

24. Louise Barry, ed., "Overland to the Goldfields of California in 1852: The Journal of John Hawkins Clark," *Kansas Historical Quarterly* 11 (August 1942): 235; "A Travel Diary in 1854 by Sarah Sutton," in Morgan, *Overland in 1846*, 7:34.

25. Osborn Cross quoted in Lewin and Taylor, *St. Joe Road*, 25.

26. "Substance of a council held between William Richardson Indian Sub Agent and the chiefs and braves of the Ioways Nation at the Great Nemaha Sub Agency on the 31st January 1850," and Mitchell to Luke Lea, February 8, 1853 (GNA, M234, roll 308).

27. Barry, *Beginning of the West*, 1130; Martha B. Caldwell, "Records of the Squatter Association of Whitehead District, Doniphan County," *Kansas Historical Quarterly* 13 (February 1944): 16–17; Herring, *Enduring Indians*, 6–9.

28. Caldwell, "Records of the Squatter Association," 18–19; Paul Wallace Gates, *Fifty Million Acres: Conflicts over Kansas Land Policy, 1854–1890* (Ithaca, NY: Atherton Press, 1966), 19; "Treaty with the Iowa, 1854," in Kappler, *Indian Affairs*, 2:628–31.

29. Gates, *Fifty Million Acres*, 11–12; Herring, *Enduring Indians*, 47.

30. Caldwell, "Records of the Squatter Association," 17, 19; Herring, *Enduring Indians*, 47; Gates, *Fifty Million Acres*, 4–5.

31. Herring, *Enduring Indians*, 1.

32. Meyer, "Iowa Indians," 287–88; Bernstein, "We Are Not Now as We Once Were," 262–63.

33. "Indian Shin Dig," *White Cloud Kansas Chief*, August 11, 1859, 2; "Great Time Among the Indians—Heap Dog!" *White Cloud Kansas Chief*, March 25, 1858, 2; "Sleigh Bells," *White Cloud Kansas Chief*, January 28, 1858, 2.

34. "Indirectly Committing Murder," *White Cloud Kansas Chief*, December 6, 1860, 2; "Disgraceful—An Indian Killed," *White Cloud Kansas Chief*, December 17, 1857, 2; Abstract, *Banks et al. v. Galbraith et al.*, 155.

35. Mahecomi quoted in Abstract, *Banks et al. v. Galbraith et al.*, 33. For more on Ioway marriage traditions, see Skinner, "Ethnology of the Ioway and Sauk Indians," 251–52.

36. "Pees-Ku-Na [?]," *White Cloud Kansas Chief*, March 29, 1860, 2; Abstract, *Banks et al. v. Galbraith et al.*, 111. For more on Ioway tattooing traditions, see Skinner, "Ethnology of the Ioway and Sauk Indians," 221, 269.

37. Irvin to Lowrie, January 13, September 13, 1853 (American Indian Correspondence, PHS, box 3); H. Craig Miner and William E. Unrau, *The End of Indian Kansas: A Study of Cultural Revolution, 1854–1871* (Lawrence: University Press of Kansas, 1977), 3, 8–13.

38. Vanderslice to Cummings, September 6, 1854 (GNA, M234, roll 308, frames 443–45).

39. Irvin to Lowrie, August 7, 1852, January 13, 1853 (American Indian Correspondence, PHS, box 3); Manypenny quoted in Herring, *Enduring Indians*, 7–8.

40. Irvin to Lowrie, August 7, 1852 (American Indian Correspondence, PHS, box 3).

41. "Treaty with the Iowa, 1854," in Kappler, *Indian Affairs*, 2:627–31; Irvin to Lowrie, August 7, 1852, February 16, 1853, and March 29, 1854 (American Indian Correspondence, PHS, box 3); Blaine, *Ioway Indians*, 246–47.

42. Daniel Vanderslice, "Report Showing the Condition of the Several Tribes Within the Great Nemaha Agency," in *Annual Report of the Bureau of Indian Affairs, 1854* (Washington, DC: Government Printing office, 1854), 307.

43. Vanderslice to Cummings, November 7, December 30, 1854, and February 6, 1857 (GNA, M234, roll 308, frames 469–70, 559–60, 587–88).

44. Attorney General's opinion quoted in *The Iowa Tribe of the Iowa Reservation in Kansas and Nebraska, The Iowa Tribe of the Iowa Reservation in Oklahoma et al. v. United States*, 20 Ind. Cl. Comm. 308 (1969), 325.

45. Vanderslice to Cummings, December 30, 1854, July 20, 1855 (GNA, M234, roll 308, frames 559–60, 700–701).

46. Caldwell, "Records of the Squatter Association," 21–22, 24, 26.

47. Ibid.; William Banks to Manypenny, November 23, 1854, and March 13, 1856 (GNA, M234, roll 308, frames 368–69, 778).

48. *Iowa Tribe v. United States* (1969), 326–27, 332.

49. Vanderslice to Cummings, April 30, June 26, 1857 (GNA, M234, roll 309, frames 130–31, 137–38); Charles E. Mix to Jacob Thompson, September 17, 1857 (GNA, M234, roll 308, frames 252–53).

50. Vanderslice to John [?] Haverly, December 2, 1857 (GNA, M234, roll 308, frame 793); Vanderslice to Cummings, January 6, 1856 (ibid., roll 309, frame 216).

51. "Notice," *White Cloud Kansas Chief*, February 4, 1858, 3; *White Cloud Kansas Chief*, January 14, 1858, 2.

52. Vanderslice to A. M. Robinson, January 21, 1860 (GNA, M234, roll 310, frame 373).

53. Ibid., January 31, 1860 (frames 382–97); ibid., May 1, 1860 (frame 434).

54. "Treaty With The Sauk and Foxes, etc., 1861. March 6, 1861," in Kappler, *Indian Affairs*, 2:811–14.

CONCLUSION

1. The epigraph is from Lance Michael Foster, e-mail message to iowayson-line@yahoogroups.com listserv, October 26, 2008.

2. *Iowa Tribe et al. v. The United States*, 327–28, 332–34. Inflation calculated on *The Inflation Calculator*, accessed June 23, 2014, http://www.westegg.com/inflation.

3. Blaine, *Ioway Indians*, 287–89.

4. See *2011 Oklahoma Indian Nations: Pocket Pictorial Dictionary* (Oklahoma City, Oklahoma Indian Affairs Commission, 2011), 16.

5. Blaine, *Ioway Indians*, 314; Lewis and Clark Bicentennial Commission, *American Indian Resource Handbook* (Jefferson City: Lewis and Clark Bicentennial Commission, 2004), 8.

6. *American Indian Resource Handbook*, 8.

7. Catlin, *Letters and Notes*, 2:30.

8. "Eagle Aviary," *Iowa Tribe of Oklahoma*, accessed June 25, 2014, www .iowanation.org/page/government/office-of-environmental-services/eagle-aviary.

Bibliography

ARCHIVAL SOURCES

American Indian Correspondence. The Presbyterian Historical Society Collection of Missionaries Letters, 1833–1893, Sac & Ioway, Sioux, Wea, 1833–64. Box 3.

Archive of Women Writers along the Rivers. Special Collections, Missouri Western State University Library, St. Joseph, Missouri.

John Dougherty Letter Book, 1826–29. State Historical Society of Missouri, Columbia.

The Iowa Tribe of the Iowa Reservation in Kansas and Nebraska, the Iowa Tribe of the Iowa Reservation in Oklahoma et al. v. United States, 20 Ind. Cl. Comm. 308 (1969).

Irvin, Samuel M. Diaries of Samuel M. Irvin. Kansas Historical Society, Microfilm MS 89.

National Archives. Great Nemaha Agency Records, 1837–76. Microfilm Publication M234, rolls 307–309, Letters Received by the Office of Indian Affairs, 1824–80. Record Group 75.

———. Ioway Subagency Records, 1825–37. Microfilm Publication M234, roll 362. Letters Received by the Office of Indian Affairs, 1824–80. Record Group 75.

———. Treaty Files. Microfilm Publication T494, roll 2. Record Group 75.

Oscar Banks et al. v. Catherine Galbraith et al. Case #8471. October term 1898. Supreme Court of Missouri. Missouri State Archives.

Vertical file, Biography: Owen, Mary Alicia, St. Joseph Public Library, St. Joseph, Missouri.

White Cloud Kansas Chief, Chronicling America, Library of Congress. http://chroniclingamerica.loc.gov.

BOOKS AND ARTICLES

Adams, David Wallace. *Education for Extinction: American Indians and the Boarding School Experience, 1875–1928*. Lawrence: University Press of Kansas, 1995.
Alex, Lynn M. *Iowa's Archaeological Past*. Iowa City: University of Iowa Press, 2000.
Anderson, Duane C. "Iowa Ethnology: A Review, Part 1." *Annals of Iowa* 41 (1973): 1228–41.
———. "Iowa Ethnology: A Review, Part 2." *Annals of Iowa* 42 (1975): 41–59.
Aron, Stephen. *American Confluence: The Missouri Frontier from Borderland to Border State*. Bloomington: Indiana University Press, 2006.
Barnes, Lela. "Notes on Imprints from Highland: The Second Point of Printing in Kansas." *Kansas Historical Quarterly* 8 (May 1939): 140–42.
Barry, Louise. *The Beginning of the West: Annals of the Kansas Gateway to the American West, 1540–1854*. Topeka: Kansas State Historical Society, 1972.
———, ed. "Overland to the Gold Fields of California in 1852: The Journal of John Hawkins Clark." *Kansas Historical Quarterly* 11 (August 1942): 227–96.
Beck, David R. M. *The Struggle for Self-Determination*. Lincoln: University of Nebraska Press, 2005.
Bernstein, David. "'We Are Not Now as We Once Were': Iowa Indians' Political and Economic Adaptations during U.S. Incorporation." *Ethnohistory* 54, no. 4 (2007): 605–37.
Blackmar, Frank W. *Kansas: A Cyclopedia of State History*. Chicago: Standard Publishing, 1912.
Blaine, Martha Royce. *The Ioway Indians*. Norman: University of Oklahoma Press, 1995.
Bradbury, John. "Bradbury's Travels." In *Early Western Travels, 1748–1846*, edited by Reuben Gold Thwaites. Vol. 5. Cleveland: Arthur H. Clark, 1905.
Caldwell, Dorothy. "The Big Neck Affair: Tragedy and Farce on the Missouri Frontier." *Missouri Historical Review* 64 (July 1970): 391–412.
Caldwell, Martha B., ed. "Records of the Squatter Association of Whitehead District, Doniphan County." *Kansas Historical Quarterly* 13 (February 1944): 16–35.
Carter, Clarence Edwin, ed. *Territorial Papers*. Vol. 15. Washington, D.C.: Government Printing Office, 1949.
Catlin, George. *Adventures of the Ojibbeway and Ioway Indians in England, France, and Belgium*. Vol. 2. 1852. Reprint. Whitefish, Mont.: Kessinger Publishing, n.d.
———. *Letters and Notes on the North American Indians*. Vol. 2. 1842. Reprint. North Dighton, Mass.: JG Press, 1995.

Chapman, Berlin Basil. "Nemaha Half-Breed Reservation." *Nebraska History* 38 (March 1957): 1–23.

Chin, Jennie, Joy Harnett, and Suzette McCord-Rogers. *Native American Heritage Museum at the Highland Mission State Historic Site.* Topeka: Kansas State Historical Society, 1996.

Clark, Charles, "W. P. Richardson." http://kansasboguslegislature.org/members /richardson_w_p.html.

Clemmons, Linda. "'We Find It a Difficult Work': Educating Dakota Children in Missionary Homes, 1835–1862." *American Indian Quarterly* 24 (Fall 2000): 570–600.

Coleman, Michael C. *American Indian Children at School, 1850–1930.* Jackson: University Press of Mississippi, 1993.

———. *Presbyterian Missionary Attitudes toward American Indians, 1837–1893.* Jackson: University Press of Mississippi, 1985.

Commissioner of Indian Affairs. *Annual Report of the Commissioner of Indian Affairs, 1849–51 to 1887.* Washington, D.C.: Government Printing Office, 1851–87.

Connelly, W. E. "Iowas, Sac/Fox of Missouri." In *Standard History of Kansas and Kansans,* 1:265–68. Chicago: Lewis Publishing, 1918.

Coy, Roy E., and Mrs. Walter Hill. "The Genealogy and History of the White Cloud Family." *Museum Graphic* 4, no. 2 (Spring 1952): 8–12.

Crosby, Alfred W. *The Columbian Exchange: Biological and Cultural Consequences of 1492.* Westport, Conn.: Greenwood, 1972.

———. *Ecological Imperialism: The Biological Expansion of Europe.* Cambridge: Cambridge University Press, 1986.

Dickey, Michael. "The Ioway Indians: Britain's Ally in the West." http://usregular0 .tripod.com/ioway.

Dorsey, James Owen. "The Social Organization of the Siouan Tribes." *Journal of American Folklore* 4 (1891): 331–42.

———. "A Study of Siouan Cults." In *Eleventh Annual Report of the Bureau of Ethnology to the Secretary of the Smithsonian Institution, 1889–1901,* 361–544. Washington, D.C.: Government Printing Office, 1894.

Dorsey, James Owen, and C. Thomas. "Iowa." *Bureau of American Ethnology Bulletin* 301, no. 1 (1907): 612–14.

Eisler, Benita. *The Red Man's Bones: George Catlin, Artist and Showman.* New York: W. W. Norton, 2013.

Everett, Derek R. "To Shed Our Blood for Our Beloved Territory: The Iowa-Missouri Borderland." *Annals of Iowa* 67 (Fall 2008): 269–97.

Fagan, Brian. *The Little Ice Age: How Climate Made History.* New York: Basic Books, 2000.

Fear-Segal, Jacqueline. *White Man's Club: Schools, Race, and the Struggle of Indian Acculturation.* Lincoln: University of Nebraska Press, 2007.

Foreman, Carolyn Thomas. "The Choctaw Academy." *Chronicles of Oklahoma* 6 (December 1928): 453–80.

Foster, Lance M. "Ancestral Ways of Life," *Ioway Cultural Institute*, http://ioway.nativeweb.org/culture/ancestrallife.htm.

——. "The Ioway and the Landscape of Southeast Iowa." *Ioway Cultural Institute*, 5. http://ioway.nativeweb.org/iowaylibrary/seiowa.htm.

——. *Sacred Bundles of the Ioway Indians.* Master's thesis, Iowa State University, 1994.

——. "Treaties." *Ioway Cultural Institute.* http://ioway.nativeweb.org/history/treaties.htm.

Fulton, A. R. *Red Men of Iowa.* Des Moines: Mills & Company, 1882.

Garraghan, G. J. *The Jesuits of the Middle United States.* Vol. 1. Chicago: Loyola University Press, 1983.

Gates, Paul Wallace. *Fifty Million Acres: Conflicts over Kansas Land Policy, 1854–1890.* Ithaca, NY: Atherton Press, 1966.

General Assembly of the Presbyterian Church. *Minutes of the General Assembly of the Presbyterian Church in the US of America, 1845–47.* Vol. 11. Philadelphia: Clerk of the General Assembly 1845–47.

GoodTracks, Jimm G. *Ioway-Otoe-Missouria Language.* www.iowayotoelang.nativeweb.org.

——. "Oral Literature Tradition." Unpublished manuscript. Collection of the author.

Gurney, George, and Therese Thau Heyman, eds. *George Catlin and His Indian Gallery.* Washington, D.C.: Smithsonian American Art Museum, 2002.

Gussow, Zachary. *An Anthropological Report: Sac, Fox and Iowa Indians.* Vol. 1. New York: Garland Press, 1974.

Hamilton, William, "Autobiography of Rev. William Hamilton." In *Transactions and Reports, Nebraska State Historical Society*, edited by Robert W. Furnas, 60–73. Lincoln, Neb.: State Journal Company, 1885.

——. "The Iowa and Sac Mission." American Indian Correspondence, Presbyterian Historical Society Collection of Missionaries' Letters, 1833–1893, box 3.

The Heritage of Buchanan County. St. Joseph: Missouri River Heritage Association, 1984.

Herring, Joseph B. *The Enduring Indians of Kansas: A Century and a Half of Acculturation.* Lawrence: University Press of Kansas, 1990.

——. "Presbyterian Ethnologists among the Iowa and Sac Indians, 1837–1853." *American Presbyterians* 65 (Fall 1987): 195–203.

——. "Selling the 'Noble Savage' Myth: George Catlin and the Iowa Indians in Europe, 1843–1845." *Kansas History: A Journal of the Central Plains* 29 (winter 2006–2007): 226–45.

Hurt, R. Douglas. *Nathan Boone and the American Frontier.* Columbia: University of Missouri Press, 1998.

Irvin, Samuel, and William Hamilton. "Iowa and Sac Tribes." In *Information Respecting the History, Conditions and Prospects of the Indian Tribes of the United States*, by Henry R. Schoolcraft. Vol. 3. Philadelphia: Lippincott, Grambo & Co., 1853.

Kappler, Charles J., ed. *Indian Affairs: Laws and Treaties*. 3 vols. Washington, D.C.: Government Printing Office, 1904.

Kurz, Rudolph Friedrich, *The Journal of Rudolph Friedrich Kurz: The Life and Work of This Swiss Artist, 1846–1852*. Edited by J. N. B. Hewitt. 1937. Reprint. Lincoln: University of Nebraska Press, 1970. Also Fairfield, Wash.: Ye Galleon Press, 1969.

Kelly, Mark William. *Lost Voices on the Missouri: John Dougherty and the Indian Frontier*. Leavenworth: Sam Clark Publishing, 2013.

Laveille, E., SJ. *The Life of Father DeSmet, SJ*. New York, P. J. Kennedy and Sons, 1915.

Lewin, Jacqueline A., and Marilyn S. Taylor. *The St. Joe Road: A Traveler's Guide from the Missouri River to the Junction of the St. Joe and Independence Roads*. St. Joseph, Mo.: St. Joseph Museum, 1992.

Lewis and Clark Bicentennial Commission. *American Indian Resource Handbook*. Jefferson City: Lewis and Clark Bicentennial Commission, 2004.

McBeth, Sally J. *Ethnic Identity and the Boarding School Experience of West Central Oklahoma American Indians*, Washington, D.C.: University Press of America, 1983.

McKenney, Thomas L., and James Hall. *History of the Indian Tribes of North America*. Vols. 1–2. Philadelphia: D. Rice & Co., 1872.

Merchant, Carolyn. *Ecological Revolutions: Nature, Gender, and Science in New England*. Chapel Hill: University of North Carolina Press, 1989.

Meyer, Roy W. "The Iowa Indians, 1836–1885." *Kansas Historical Quarterly* 29 (1962): 273–300.

Miles, William. "Enamored with Colonization: Isaac McCoy's Plan of Indian Reform." *Kansas Historical Quarterly* 38 (Autumn 1972): 268–86.

Miner, H. Craig, and William E. Unrau. *The End of Indian Kansas: A Study of Cultural Revolution, 1854–1871*. Lawrence: University Press of Kansas, 1977.

Morgan, Dale. *Overland in 1846: Diaries and Letters of the California-Oregon Trail*. Lincoln: University of Nebraska Press, 1993.

Morgan, Lewis Henry. *The Indian Journals, 1859–62*. Edited by Leslie A. White. Ann Arbor: University of Michigan Press, 1959.

Newcomb, Steve. "Five Hundred Years of Injustice: The Legacy of Fifteenth Century Injustice," *Indigenous Law Institute*. http://ili.nativeweb.org/sdrm_art .html.

Oklahoma Indian Affairs Commission. *2011 Oklahoma Indian Nations: Pocket Pictorial Dictionary*. Oklahoma City: Oklahoma Indian Affairs Commission, 2011.

Olson, Greg. *The Ioway in Missouri*. Columbia: University of Missouri Press, 2008.

———. "Navigating the White Road: White Cloud's Struggle to Lead the Ioway along the Path of Acculturation." *Missouri Historical Review* 99 (January 2005): 93–114.

———. "Slave, Trader, Interpreter, and World Traveler: The Remarkable Life of Jeffrey Deroine." *Missouri Historical Review* 107 (July 2013): 222–30.

———. "Two Portraits, Two Legacies: Anglo-American Artists View Chief White Cloud." *Gateway* 25 (summer 2005): 21–31.

———. *Voodoo Priests, Noble Savages, and Ozark Gypsies: The Life of Folklorist Mary Alicia Owen.* Columbia: University of Missouri Press, 2012.

Peterson, Cindy, ed. *Archaeological Study of Iowaville, a 1765–1824 Ioway (Báxoje) Village in Van Buren County, Iowa.* Iowa City: Office of the State Archaeologist, 2012.

Plank, Pryor. "The Ioway, Sac and Fox Indian Mission and Its Missionaries, Rev. Samuel Irvin and Wife." In *Transactions of the Kansas State Historical Society, 1907–1908,* 10:312–25. Topeka: Kansas State Historical Society, 1908.

Presbyterian Board of Foreign Missionaries. *Annual Reports of the Presbyterian Board of Foreign Missionaries.* New York: Presbyterian Church of the United States of America, Board of Foreign Missionaries, 1838–48.

Prucha, Francis Paul. *The Indians in American Society: From the Revolutionary War to the Present.* Berkeley: University of California Press, 1985.

Rankin, William. "Rev. William Hamilton," and "Rev. Samuel M. and Mrs. Irvin." *Memorials of Foreign Missionaries of the Presbyterian Church, U.S.A.* Philadelphia: Presbyterian Board of Publications and Sabbath-School Work, 1895.

Rollings, Willard H. *The Osage: An Ethnocentrical Study of Hegemony on the Prairie-Plains.* Columbia: University of Missouri Press, 1992.

———. *Unaffected by the Gospel: Osage Resistance to the Christian Invasion, 1673–1906: A Cultural Victory.* Albuquerque: University of New Mexico Press, 2004.

Schoolcraft, Henry R. *Information Respecting the History, Conditions and Prospects of the Indian Tribes of the United States.* Vol. 3. Philadelphia: Lippincott, Grambo & Co., 1853.

Schusky, Ernest L. "The Upper Missouri Indian Agency, 1819–1868." *Missouri Historical Review* 65 (April 1971): 249–69.

Schwartz, Saul. "Iowaville Historic Context." In *Archaeological Study of Iowaville, a 1765–1824 Ioway (Báxoje) Village in Van Buren County, Iowa,* edited by Cindy Peterson, 4–29. Iowa City: Office of the State Archaeologist, 2012.

———. "Iowaville in Perspectives: Expansive Ethnohistory at an Ioway Indian Village." Honors thesis, Beloit College, 2008.

Shultz, George A. *An Indian Canaan: Isaac McCoy and the Vision of an Indian State.* Norman: University of Oklahoma Press, 1972.

Skinner, Alanson. "Ethnology of the Ioway and Sauk Indians." *Bulletin of the Public Museum of the City of Milwaukee* 5 (1923–26).

———. "Societies of the Iowa, Kansas and Ponca Indians." *Anthropological Papers of the American Museum of Natural History* 11 (1915): 685–739.

———. "Traditions of the Iowa Indians." *Journal of American Folklore* 38 (October–December 1925): 427–506.

Stevens, Frank E. *The Black Hawk War.* Chicago: Frank E. Stevens, 1903.

Stevenson, Winona. "Beggars, Chickabobbooags, and Prisons: Paxoche (Ioway) Views of English Society, 1844–45." *American Indian Culture and Research Journal* 17, no. 4 (1993): 1–23.

Taylor, Bayard. *Views Afoot: Or, Europe Seen with Knapsack and Staff.* 1846. Reprint. The Literature Network, http://www.online-literature.com/bayard-taylor/views -a-foot/1.

Taylor, Theodore W. *The Bureau of Indian Affairs.* Boulder, Colo.: Westview Press, 1984.

Theler, James L., and Robert F. Boszhardt. *Twelve Millennia: Archaeology of the Upper Mississippi River Valley.* Iowa City: University of Iowa Press, 2003.

Thorne, Tanis C. *The Many Hands of My Relations: French and Indians on the Lower Missouri.* Columbia: University of Missouri Press, 1996.

Unrau, William E. *The Rise and Fall of Indian Country, 1825–1855.* Lawrence: University Press of Kansas, 2007.

"Walter Lowrie, Secretary of the Senate, 1825–1836." *Art and History, U.S. Senate.* http://www.senate.gov/artandhistory/history/common/generic/SOS_Walter _Lowrie.htm.

Warhus, Mark. *Another America: Native American Maps and the History of Our Land.* New York: St. Martin's Press, 1997.

Wedel, Mildred Mott. "Peering at the Ioway Indians through the Mist of Time, 1650–c. 1700," *Journal of the Iowa Archeological Society* 33 (1986): 1–74.

Werner, Morris W. "Indian Missions in Kansas." *Kansas Heritage.* Accessed March 12, 2014. http://www.kansasheritage.org/werner/mission.html.

Wilhelm, Paul, duke of Wurttemberg. *Travels in North America, 1822–1824.* Translated by W. Robert Nitske. Edited by Savoie Lottinville. Norman: University of Oklahoma Press, 1973.

Wilkins, David E. *American Indian Politics and the American Political System.* Lanham, Md.: Rowman and Littlefield, 1997.

Wilkins, David, and K. Tsianina Lomawaima. *Uneven Ground: Indian Sovereignty and Federal Law.* Norman: University of Oklahoma Press, 2001.

Willoughby, Robert J. *The Brothers Robidoux and the Opening of the American West.* Columbia: University of Missouri Press, 2012.

———. *Robidoux's Town: A Nineteenth-Century History of St. Joseph, Missouri.* Westphalia, Mo.: Westphalia Printing, 1997.

Index

References to illustrations are in italic type.

Adams, David Wallace, 58–59
Adams, John Quincy (U.S. pres.), 84
agriculture, 18
Algonquin language, 4, 7, 28
allotment, 113, 117–18
Always Dancing (WašíMáñi, Fast
    Dancer, or Jim) (Ioway): in Europe,
    32, 100; name, 132n37
André, Father Louis (missionary), 4, 17
Anenein (Ioway girl), 62
Arikaras, 8
Atchison, David Rice (Mo. sen.), 91

Ballard, Aurey (missionary), 20–21, 29
Bangs, Mr. (Ioway Agency farmer), 67
Banks, Joseph (son of William Banks
    and Giant Woman, student at
    mission school), 51
Banks, William (farmer and
    merchant), 51, 62, 116
Baptists, 41
Barbour, James (sec. of war), 80

Barnum, P. T., 100, 103
Báxoje. *See* Ioways (Báxoje)
Bean, Jonathan (Indian agent), 71–72;
    report on the Great Nemaha
    Subagency, 85–86
beings (*wan^shinge*), 18
Bellevue Agency, Neb. *See* Upper
    Missouri Indian Agency
Benton, Thomas Hart (Mo. sen.), 15,
    84–85
Bernstein, David, 100–101, 104, 111
Big Neck. *See* Great Walker (MáñiXáñe,
    Moanahonga, or Big Neck) (Ioway
    headman)
Big Sioux River, 6
Blackfeet, 49, 56
Black Hawk (Sac and Fox headman), 10
Blaine, Martha Royce, 61–62
Blistered Feet (ThíNádaye or See-
    mon-ty-a) (Ioway medicine man): in
    Europe, 33–35, *34*; name, 133n42
Blood Run (Good Earth State Park), 4

Bloohm, Paul (missionary), 104
Boggs, Lilburn (Missouri governor), 84
Boilvin, Nicolas (Indian agent), 9
Bradley, Henry (mission school
    teacher), 24, 42
Britain, 9–10, 63
British (Ragrášhe) (Ioway headman),
    76, 77, 113; names, 138n46; picked
    to succeed No Heart, 79–80
Brown, Orlando (comm. of Indian
    Affairs), 93
Burbank, John A. (Great Nemaha
    agent), 79–80, 111
Bureau of Indian Affairs, 29, 43–44,
    56, 70, 95, 115, 123; corruption
    81–97; land sales in the Kansas
    Territory, 117; reorganization,
    93–94, 139n1
Busy Man (Ioway), 99

Calhoun, John C. (sec. of war), 11
California gold rush, 105
Campbell, James (mixed-blood
    Ioway), 75
Campbell, Sophia (student at mission
    school), 56
Campbell, William (student at mission
    school), 51
Caromonga. See Clearing Sky
    (Kéramañi or Caromonga) (Ioway
    headman)
Cass, Lewis (Mich. terr. gov.), 13
Catlin, George, 32–35, 98–104, 124
Chariton River, Mo., 7, 8, 9, 10, 12
Cherokees, 20
Cheyennes, 50
Childs, Mary (student at mission
    school), 56
Chippewa and Ottawa Mission, Mich.,
    41, 43
Choctaw Academy, Ky., 40–41
Choctaw Mission, Kans., 37
Choctaws, 20

Chouteau, Auguste (trader), 10
Christianity, 17–36
Christian missionaries, 19–22; funded
    by U.S. Congress, 41
Christian schools, 39–41
Clark, James Hawkins (emigrant),
    107–108
Clark, William (Mo. terr. gov.,
    superint. of Indian affairs), 9, 10,
    11, 13, 40, 70, 80, 84; death, 82–84
Clearing Sky (Kéramañi or
    Caromonga) (Ioway headman), 72;
    name, 138n33
Clemmons, Linda, 57–58
Coleman, Michael, 21–24
Commanding General, the
    (Wéxawìrugra^n or Wa-ta-we-bu-
    ka-na) (son of Raining): in Europe,
    32, 100; name, 133n38
Cooke, C. W. (emigrant), 107
Cooper's Fort, Mo., 9
Corsair (Pirate) (son of Little Wolf and
    She Herself Follows On): death,
    104; in Europe, 100
Cote Sans Dessein, Mo., 9
Crane (Pécha^n) (Ioway headman),
    13–14
Crawford, T. Hartley (comm. of
    Indian affairs), 85, 87
Creator of the Earth (Ma$^\wedge$un), 68; in
    Ioway spirituality, 17
Cross, Osborn (emigrant), 108
Crowell, David (student at mission
    school), 49
Cruthers, Lizza (student at mission
    school), 56
Cummings, Alfred (superint. of
    Indian affairs), 115
Cushing, Caleb (U.S. attorney gen.),
    115

Dakota Sioux, 6, 8, 9, 57, 63, 64, 65
Davis, Sarah (emigrant), 106

Dawes Act, 114, 120, 122–23
Delawares (people), 41
Denver, I. W. (comm. of Indian affairs), 117
Democratic Party, 88–89, 91
Department of the Interior, 93
Department of War, 93
Deroine, Jeffrey (Ioway interpreter, trader), 28, 72; dismissal, 73–74, 88; in Europe, 100–104
Descartes, René, 19
DeSmet, Father Pierre-Jean, 40
Des Moines River, 7, 9, 10
Dickens, Charles, 101
Discovery Doctrine, 128n6
Doctor, the. *See* Blistered Feet (ThíNádaye or See-mon-ty-a) (Ioway medicine man)
Doniphan County, Kans., 82
Doré. *See* Twin Holy Boys (Doré and Wahrédua)
Dorian, Elisha (Ioway interpreter), 73
Dougherty, John (Indian agent), 67, 69, 71, 72, 81–85
Douglas, Stephen A. (Ill. sen.), 109
Dupee, Francis (student at mission school), 52
Dyche, James (Doniphan Co., Kans., resident), 112

Earth clans, 60–61
Eaton, John (sec. of war), 15
Eddy, Norman (special comm. of land sales), 117
Edwards, Ninian (Ill. terr. gov.), 10
emigrants (on Oregon Trail): accounts of Ioways, 106–108; allegations of kidnapping, 106–107; vandalism, 107
Ewing, Thomas (sec. of the interior), 93

Fast Dancer. *See* Always Dancing (WašíMáñi, Fast Dancer, or Jim) (Ioway)

Foreman, Harvey (agency farmer), 119
Foreman, John (agency farmer, trader), 89–90, 94; land dealings, 95–96
Fort Leavenworth, Kans., 15
Foster, Lance, 121
France, 8, 63
Fulton, A. R., 10

Gatling, Richard (cofounder of White Cloud, Kans.), 111
Geiger, Vincent (emigrant), 107
General Land Office, 82, 110
George III (king of England), 63
Giants (Waru'ska), 31, 37
Giant Woman (Waru'skami) (Ioway) (wife of William Banks), 51, 62
Gibson, George R. (attorney), 90–91
Gilmore, James (trader), 70
Good Earth State Park. *See* Blood Run (Good Earth State Park)
GoodTracks, Jimm, 4, 39
Grand River, Mo., 7, 8, 9, 10
Great Nemaha River, 15
Great Nemaha Subagency/Agency, 15, *83, 115, 119*; becomes a full agency, 94, 127n1; establishment of, 20–21, 82–83; mismanagement of, 71, 81–97; and the Oregon Trail, 105–109; reduction in size, 54–57, 95, 109–11, 113, 119
Great Walker (MáñiXáñe, Moanahonga, or Big Neck) (Ioway headman), 11–13, 20, 64
Green Bay, Wisc., 3, 4, 6, 17, 61
Greenwood, Albert (comm. of Indian Affairs), 56
Grey Snow Eagle House (Bah Kho-je Xla Chi), 124
Gussow, Zachary, 8

Haldimand, Frederick (British colonial gov.), 63

Hall, Ann Richardson (daughter of
    William Richardson; wife of
    Willard P. Hall), 93
Hall, Samuel C. (St. Joseph
    Democratic politician), 91
Hall, Willard P. (Mo. gov.), 93
Hamilton, Joseph V. (Indian agent),
    71, 85
Hamilton, Julia Ann McGiffin
    (missionary; wife of William
    Hamilton), 21, 46
Hamilton, William (missionary):
    arrival in Kansas, 21–22; assessment
    of Ioway leaders, 76; attempts to
    convert the Ioways, 23–26; life after
    missions closure, 57; plan to expand
    the mission, 54; political influence,
    86–87, 90–92, 94; reports on
    mission school, 49; as schoolteacher
    30–31, 36; support for subagents,
    91–93; use of the Ioways' language,
    28–30
Hard Heart (WayíⁿWèxa or
    Wyingwaha) (Ioway headman),
    9–10, 63
Hardy, Rosetta (mission school
    teacher), 41, 43
Harris, Carey (comm. of Indian
    Affairs), 82, 84
Harrison, William Henry (gen., U.S.
    pres.), 8, 87, 93
Harvey, Thomas (superint. of Indian
    Affairs), 47, 72–73, 75, 89, 93; in
    council with Ioways, 74, 89–91;
    Ioways' complaints about, 92
Hears Intermittently (Náx^úⁿMáñi,
    No-ho-mun-ya, Roman Nose, or the
    War Chief) (Ioway): on Christianity,
    32–33; death of, 104; in Europe,
    100; name, 141n5
Henderson, Nancy (mission school
    teacher), 20, 26, 41
Herring, Joseph B., 100, 104, 111

Hewathoche (Ioway headman), 28
Highland, Kans., 26, 124
Hobbes, Thomas, 19
Horton, Azariah (missionary), 20
Hughes, Andrew S. (Ioway subagent),
    15, 65, 67–68; charges of fraud
    against, 81–86; dismissal, 71
Hughes, Bella (daughter of Andrew
    Hughes), 90
Hughes, James M. (Mo. congressman),
    88, 91
Hughes, William (trader), 94–95
Huntsville, Mo., 13
Hutchens, James (emigrant), 107
Hu-toy (Lowry) (Ioway), 79

Illinois (people), 4
Illinois (terr./state), 3, 7, 10
Independence, Mo., 105
Indian Civilization Fund, 41
Indian Claims Commission, 121–22
Indian reform policies, 11, 80
Indian Reorganization Act, 80
Intercourse Act of 1834, 70
Iowa (territory/state), 3, 4, 6, 7, 12–13,
    84; border dispute with Missouri, 13
Iowa Point, Kans., 26, 51, 96; as a
    source of alcohol, 72
Iowa River, 7
Iowa Tribe of Kansas and Nebraska,
    123–25
Iowa Tribe of Oklahoma, 122–25
Iowaville (Iowa), 7, 10
Ioway (Iowa), Sac and Fox Mission:
    church, 26; closure of, 55–57;
    establishment of, 20–26; failure of,
    57–59; school buildings, 24, 28,
    42–49, 45, 124; school curriculum,
    49–51; staff, 42–43; students, 52–54
Ioway Agency, Mo., 12, 41
Ioways (Báxoje): acculturation, 67–68,
    111–13, 117–18; acquisition of the
    horse, 6; alcohol use, 35, 72–73, 79,

112, 114; battles with Sacs and
Foxes, 10; battles with the United
States, 9–10, 12–13; clan system, 14,
18, 60–61, 123; debt and poverty of,
71, 78, 95–97, 101, 114, 117;
descriptions of, 100, 106; disease
among, 9, 46, 58, 76–78, 105,
129n15; early history, 3–18; and
emigrants, 105–109; in Europe,
31–36, 98–104, *103*; farming, 18,
111, 123–24; internment practices,
106; marriage, 61–63, 112; meaning
of the name, 4; move to Indian
Territory, 119–20, 122; population,
58, 69, 76, 122–23; removal from
Missouri, 104; resistance to
Christianity, 30–31, 35, 57–59;
sacred bundles and pipes
(*ráhnuwes*), 31–32; spirituality,
17–36; support for mission school,
44–47, 58; traditional education,
37–40; traditional leadership,
60–61, 80; traditional stories, 31,
38–39; treaties with the United
States, 8, 10–16, 68–69, 84, 95, 110,
112–14, 119; village locations, 4, *5*,
6–10, 17, 24, 26, *27*, 28, 78, 82
Ioway Tribal Historic Preservation
Office, 125
Ioway Tribal Museum and Cultural
Heritage Center (Báxoje Wósgaci),
125
Irvin, Eliza (missionary; wife of
Samuel Irvin), 21, *23*
Irvin, Francis (mission farmer;
brother of Samuel Irvin), 26
Irvin, Samuel (missionary), *23*, 78;
arrival in Kansas, 21–22; attempts
to convert the Ioways, 23–26,
30–31, 36; concerns about Ioways'
trip to Europe, 101–102; as Ioway
interpreter, 139n10; land dealings,
96; life after missions closure, 57;

opposition to allotment, 113; plan
to expand the mission, 54; political
influence, 86–87, 90–92, 94;
quoted, 17, 29; reports on mission
school, 50, 52, 56; support for
subagents, 91–93; use of the Ioways'
language, 28–30
Ishjinki, 37–38

Jackson, Andrew (U.S. pres.),
68–69, 84
Jackson, Congrave (Great Nemaha
subagent), 42, 87
Jefferson, Thomas (U.S. pres.),
63–64
Jim. *See* Always Dancing (WašíMáñi,
Fast Dancer, or Jim) (Ioway)
Johnson, Richard Mentor (founder of
Choctaw Academy), 40
Johnson, Sarah Davis (missionary;
wife of Thomas Johnson), 41
Johnson, Thomas (missionary), 41
Johnson v. McIntosh, 128n6
Jordan, James H. (trader), 10

Kansas City, Mo., 14
Kansas-Nebraska Act, 14, 95, 109–10
Kansas State Historical Society, 124
Kansas Territory; 94; creation of,
109–10
Kaws, 7, 8
Kearney, Stephen Watts (gen.), 15
Kelly, John W. (attorney), 74, 92
Keokuk (Sac and Fox headman), 84
Keyes, Charles R., 3
Kickapoo Academy, Kans., 44,
134n20
Kickapoos, 41, 94
Kirksville, Mo., 12
Kirusche (Ioway headman; father of
Witthae), 62
Kurz, Rudolph Friedrich (artist), 40,
62, 78

Laclede, Pierre (trader, founder of St. Louis), 6–7

Laggarash. *See* British (Ragrášhe) (Ioway headman)

Lakota Sioux, 6

La Salle, René-Robert Cavalier, sieur de (explorer), 6, 128n6

Lea, Luke (comm. of Indian Affairs), 109

Lee, Fanny (student at mission school), 51

Le Voleur. *See* Thief, the (Wamúnu or Le Voleur) (Ioway headman; not to be confused with Man Who Steals)

Lewis (son of Raining; student at mission school), 51

Linn, Lewis (Mo. sen.), 15

Lisa, Manual (trader, Indian agent), 9

Little Wolf (Ioway headman), 74, 76, 113; in Europe, 100

Liverpool, England, 32, 99

London, England, 33, 100–103

Louisiana Purchase, 8

Louis-Philippe (king of France), 102, *103*

Lowrie, Walter (BFM sec.), 22–23, 28; correspondence with Irvin and Hamilton, 49–50, 56, 96

Madison, James (U.S. pres.), 10

Mahaskah. *See* White Cloud (MaxúThka or Mahaskah) (Ioway headman)

Ma-hee, John (Ioway), 79

Manifest Destiny, 19

Man Who Steals (Wamúnu) (Ioway headman, not to be confused with the Thief), 76, 115, 138n46

Manypenny, George (comm. of Indian Affairs), 78, 94, 113, 116

Marcy, William (sec. of war), 90, 92

Marshall, James (discover of gold at Sutter's Mill, Calif.), 105

Marshall, John (chief justice), 128n6

Mascoutins, 6, 7

McClintock, Armstrong (Great Nemaha subagent), 89–91

McClintock, Hugh (agency farmer; brother of Armstrong McClintock), 89

McCoy, Isaac (missionary, surveyor), 24, 26, 41; complaints about, 82–83, 115

McKenney, Thomas L. (comm. of Indian Affairs), 11, 65, 67

McKinney, Edward (missionary), 54

mechanistic consciousness, 18–19

Medill, William (comm. of Indian Affairs), 89–91

Melody, George Henry Curzon (promoter), 100–103

Membre, Father Zenobius (missionary), 4

Merchant, Carolyn, 18–19

Methodists: founding missions in Kansas, 41; invited to the Great Nemaha Agency, 56

Meyer, Andrew (agency blacksmith), 89

Meyer, Roy W., 104, 111

Miami County, Kans., 20

Miller, Sol (publisher of *White Cloud Kansas Chief*), 78–79, 111

Minnesota, 3, 4, 6

Mission Creek, Kans. (Iowa Branch), 24

Mississippi River, 6–9

Missouri (territory/state), 7, 8, 9, 10, 11, 14; Ioway rights to land in, 11–15, 64–69, 98; northern border, 12–13; politics, 82–85, 88–93, 104; western border, 13–15, 68, 104

Missourias, 3, 7, 8

Missouri Compromise of 1820, 109

Missouri General Assembly, 15

Missouri River: as boundary between settlers and Natives, 12–15, 58, 64, 67–73, 104–105; emigrants crossing, 105, 108; as trade route, 72

Mitchell, David D. (superint. of Indian Affairs), 87, 94, 109
Moanahonga. *See* Great Walker (MániXáñe, Moanahonga, or Big Neck) (Ioway headman)
Monroe, James, 11
Monroe County, Mo., 8
Morgan, Lewis Henry (ethnographer), 97
Mother Earth (Hina Maya), 18
Murray, Kirwin (student at mission school), 52, 53

Naggarash. *See* British (Ragráshe) (Ioway headman)
Native American Graves Protection and Repatriation Act (NAGPRA), 125
Native American Heritage Museum, 124
Nemaha Half-Breed Reservation, Neb., 14, 51
Nesoquat (Sac headman), 28
Neumonya. *See* Raining (Ñi'yuMa'ñi, Neumonya, or Walking Rain) (Ioway headman)
Newton, Sir Isaac, 19
Nicholas V (pope), 128n6
Noble Savage, 102
No Heart (Na'hjeNing'e or Notchimine) (Ioway headman), 28, 37, 42, 43, 66, 71, 75, 90; advisor to Francis White Cloud, 65–69; complaints about the Oregon Trail, 108; death of, 79; as Ioway head chief, 75–76; role in treaty making, 69, 112–13; views regarding the boarding school, 44, 58–59
Noheart, Eliza (student at mission school), 56
No-ho-mun-ya. *See* Hears Intermittently (Náx^úⁿMáñi, No-ho-mun-ya, Roman Nose, or the War Chief) (Ioway)

Notchimine. *See* No Heart (Na'hjeNing'e or Notchimine) (Ioway headman)

O'Fallon, Benjamin (Indian agent), 64
Ojibwas, 13, 99
Oke-we-me. *See* She Herself Follows On (AkúweMi or Oke-we-mi) (wife of Little Wolf)
Old Pete (whiskey trader), 79
Omaha (people), 6, 8, 9, 14, 43, 54; conflict with the Ioways, 64–65
Omaha, Neb., 6
Oneida, 3
Oneota, 3–4, 12
Orator, the (Waích^eMáñi or the War Leader) (Ioway headman), 8, 67, 69
Oregon Trail, 114; as a source of conflict, 76, 105–109
Orr, Ellison, 3
Osages, 8; conflict with Ioways, 9
Osage Subagency, Kans., 87
Otoe and Omaha Mission, Neb., 52, 54, 56, 57
Otoes, 3, 6, 7, 14, 51, 54; at the mission school, 49; relations with the Ioways, 64, 76
Owen, Mary Alicia (folklorist), 106
Oxford (sailing packet), 32, 99–100

Paris, France, 35, 102–104
participatory consciousness, 18–19
Pashepaho (Sac and Fox headman), 10
Pawnees: Francis White Cloud's attack against, 75; at the missions school, 56
peace medals, 63–64
Perkins, Okla., 122
Peter (son of Great Walker), 20
Pettis, Spencer (Mo. congressman), 15
Pierce, Franklin (U.S. pres.), 94
Pilcher, Joshua (superint. of Indian Affairs), 82–85, 87
Pittsburg, Penn., 22

plantain (white man's foot), 68
Platte Purchase. *See* Treaty of 1836 (Platte Purchase)
Platte River, Mo., 7, 10, 12, 13, 15, 67–68
Platte River, Neb., 6
Plum (Káⁿje) (Ioway headman), 28, 30
Poinsett, Joel Roberts (sec. of war), 82
Polk, James K. (U.S. pres.), 88
Poncas, 9
"Poor Lucy" (Mary Alicia Owen story), 106
popular sovereignty, 109–10
Portage de Sioux, 10
Porter, J. M. (sec. of war), 100
Prairie du Chien, Wisc., 7, 13, 64
Preemption Law of 1841, 110, 115
Presbyterian Board of Foreign Missionaries (BFM), 23, 28–29; approach to education, 37; assigning names to mission school students, 49–50; establishing and supporting schools, 41, 43–44, 49; land grant, 95–96; purpose and goals, 20–22
Presbyterian Church of the United States of America (PCUSA), 20, 44
Prophet, the (Iowa who traveled to Europe), 32
Pumpkin (Wadwáⁿ) (Ioway leader), 28, 67

Rabbit (Mischinye), 37
Raining (Ñi'yuMa'ñi, Neumonya, or Walking Rain) (Ioway headman), 13, 26–28, 69, 71, 75; in Europe, 32; name, 130n29; on religion, 33; views regarding the boarding school, 44
Ramsey, James B. (missionary), 37
Rankin, Arthur (promoter), 99
Red Earth (MayaⁿShuje), 3
Richardson, William (Great Nemaha subagent/agent): accusations against

Jeffrey Deroine, 73–74; campaign to be reinstated as subagent, 93–94; in council with Ioways, 71, 73, 108; description of, 87; resignation, 88–89; subagency map made by, 26, 27, 28, 42, 78; support for mission school, 44
Robidioux, Sylvania (student at mission school), 51
Robidoux, Angelique (wife of Joseph Robidoux), 61
Robidoux, Joseph (trader; founder of St. Joseph, Mo.), 70, 94–95; father of Ioway children, 61–62; owner of Jeffrey Deroine, 74
Robidoux, Mary (daughter of Joseph Robidoux; wife of Francis White Cloud), 62
Robinson, Joseph, A. M. (superint. of Indian Affairs), 118
Rollings, Willard, 19, 35
Roman Nose. *See* Hears Intermittently (Náx^úⁿMáñi, No-ho-mun-ya, Roman Nose, or the War Chief) (Ioway)
Roy, John Baptiste (Ioway interpreter), 75; death, 52; land grant, 95
Rucker, William (Great Nemaha subagent), 47, 74–75, 91–93

Sacs and Foxes, 13, 63, 108; disease among, 46, 78; early relations with Ioways, 7–11; move to Indian Territory, 122; of the Mississippi, 68–69, 76, 84; of the Missouri, 12, 15, 22, 24, 72; population, 69; resistance to missionaries, 28–30, 41–44, 46–47, 49, 54, 57; sharing agency with Ioways, 26, 46, 54–55, 67–68, 82, 86, 94–97, 104, 108, 111, 122; struggle to keep land in Kansas, 111–20
Salt River, 8

Sand, George (French writer), 102
Santee Sioux, 14
Schusky, Earnest, 92
Schuyler County, Mo., 12
Schwartz, Saul, 7
Second Great Awakening, 19–20
See-non-ty-a. *See* Blistered Feet
 (ThíNádaye or See-mon-ty-a)
 (Ioway medicine man)
settlers: in the Kansas Territory, 105–20;
 perceptions of Ioways, 111–12
Sharp Elbows (Ihdo'pahin), 31, 37
Shawnee Methodist Mission,
 Kans., 41
Shawnees, 41
She Herself Follows on (AkúweMi or
 Oke-we-mi) (wife of Little Wolf):
 death of, 104; in Europe, 100
Sheppard, E. M. (missionary), 20
Shokape (Sac headman), 28
Shooting Cedar (Ioway), 99
Sioux (people), 8, 13; at the mission
 school, 49, 56
Sioux Falls, S.Dak., 4
Sky clans, 60–61
slavery, 109, 110
Smith, Elisha P. (Ioway interpreter), 29
Spain, 63
Spirit Lake, Ia., 4
squatters: chance to purchase claims,
 117; in the Kansas Territory,
 109–11, 116, 122
squatters' associations, 116
St. Joseph, Mo., 78, 89, 93, 96; as a
 stop on the Oregon Trail, 105
St. Joseph Gazette, 78, 116
St. Louis, Mo., 99
St. Regis School, Mo., 20, 40
Striker Creek, Kans., 24
Strutting Pigeon Woman
 (Rúúht^ánweMi) (wife of Francis
 White Cloud): in Europe, 100;
 name, 141n5

Supreme Being (Wakanda), 17
Sutter's Mill, Calif., 105
Sutton, Sarah (emigrant), 106, 108

Taylor, Bayard (writer), 31–32,
 99–100
Taylor, Zachary (U.S. pres.), 93
Thief, the (Wamúnu or Le Voleur)
 (Ioway headman; not to be
 confused with Man Who Steals), 63,
 136n11
Thorne, Tanis, 14
Thunder Beings, 17
trade: British, 9; fraud, 84, 92,
 94–95; French, 6, 7, 17; United
 States, 10, 70, 86; used to disrupt
 Ioway leadership, 62–64; whiskey,
 11, 42, 72–73, 79, 83, 87–88,
 92, 112
Trade and Intercourse Acts of
 1804, 72
traders: Ioways' debt to, 71–73, 101,
 117; relations with the Ioways, 14,
 61–64, 70, 79, 94–95
Treaty of 1805, 8
Treaty of 1815, 10
Treaty of 1824, 11–12
Treaty of 1830, 13–14
Treaty of 1836 (Platte Purchase),
 14–16, 68, 96, 104
Treaty of 1837, 69, 84
Treaty of 1854, 55–56, 95, 110–14;
 and land fraud, 96–97; restitution,
 121–22
Treaty of 1861, 119
Twin Holy Boys (Doré and
 Wahrédua), 31, 37
Tyler, John (U.S. pres.), 87, 93

United States: and exertion of
 influence in Ioway leadership,
 63–65; mismanagement of the
 terms of the Treaty of 1854, 121

United States Congress, 15, 94; House
    Committee on Indian Affairs, 41;
    and the Kansas-Nebraska Act, 95,
    109–10
United States Fish and Wildlife
    Service, 125
United States Senate, 22, 110
United States Supreme Court, 13;
    Johnson v. McIntosh, 128n6
Upper Iowa River, 3, 4, 7, 8
Upper Missouri Indian Agency, 71,
    81, 85, 93

Van Buren, Martin (U.S. pres.), 82, 87
Van Buren County, Iowa, 7, 15
Vanderslice, Daniel (Great Nemaha
    agent), 52, 56, 94; allegations of
    land fraud, 96–97; reports on the
    Ioways, 78; support for allotment,
    113–15, 117–18; struggle with
    squatters, 116–19; Treaty of 1854
    negotiations, 95
Vanderslice, Thomas (son of David
    Vanderslice), 116
Van Quickenborne, Father Charles
    Felix (headmaster at St. Regis),
    20, 40
Vasques, Gabriel (Indian agent), 20
Vaughan, Alfred J. (Great Nemaha
    subagent), 92–93
Voi Ri Gran (Ioway headman), 8

Wabasha (Mdewakaton Sioux
    headman), 14
Wahrédua. *See* Twin Holy Boys (Doré
    and Wahrédua)
Walking Rain. *See* Raining (Ñi'yuMa'ñi,
    Neumonya, or Walking Rain)
    (Ioway headman)
Wallace, Harriet (mission church
    parishioner), 26
War Chief, the. *See* Hears
    Intermittently (Náx^ú^nMáñi,

No-ho-mun-ya, Roman Nose, or the
    War Chief) (Ioway)
War Leader, the. *See* Orator, the
    (Waích^eMáñi or the War Leader)
    (Ioway headman)
War of 1812, 9–10
Washington, D.C., Ioways in, 84
Washkamonya. *See* Always Dancing
    (WašíMáñi, Fast Dancer, or Jim)
    (Ioway)
Wa-ta-we-bu-ka-na. *See* Commanding
    General, the (Wéxawìrugra^n or
    Wa-ta-we-bu-ka-na) (son of Raining)
Wea and Piankeshaw Mission, Kans.,
    20, 41, 43
Wekan stories, 38–39
Whig party, 87, 93; in Great Nemaha
    Subagency politics, 84, 89
White Cloud (MaxúThka or
    Mahaskah) (Ioway headman),
    11–14, 20, 40, 42, 64–67
White Cloud, Francis (Ioway
    headman), 28, *48*, 90; accusation
    against missionaries, 47, 74–75;
    attack against Pawnees, 75;
    disagreements with William
    Richardson, 87–88; dissatisfaction
    over annuities, 70–72; in Europe,
    32, 74, 100–104; as headman,
    65–67; and Jeffrey Deroine, 73–74;
    marriage, 62; move to the Nemaha
    River, 51; role in treaty making,
    68–69; stripped of power, 74–76
White Cloud, James (Ioway headman),
    123
White Cloud, Kans., 80, 111, 123
White Cloud, Robert (son of Francis
    White Cloud), 79
White Cloud, Sophia (daughter of
    Francis White Cloud and Strutting
    Pigeon Woman), in Europe, 100
White Cloud, William (student at
    mission school), 51

White Cloud Kansas Chief, 78–79, 111, 118
White Crow (KáxeThka) (Ioway headman), 30
White Crow, Charles (student at mission school), 51
Whitehead, James R. (trader), 116
white man's foot. *See* plantain (white man's foot)
Wilkinson, James (gen., territorial gov.), 8
Wilson, Mrs. (Mahecomi) (Ioway), 112
Winnebagos, 3, 13, 17, 63

Witthae (daughter of Kirusche), 62
Wolf Grove, Kans., 95–96
Wolf River, Kans., 24, *25*, 26; emigrants crossing, 107–108
Worage stories, 38–39
Wounding Arrow (MáHége) (Ioway headman; father of White Cloud), 65

Yankton Dakotas, 14, 64
Yanktoni Dakotas, 9
Yellowstone (steamboat), 99
York, England, 33